*The*
# HUMANITARIAN
# LEADER *in Each of Us*

*Also by Frank LaFasto and Carl Larson*

Teamwork: What Must Go Right/What Can Go Wrong

When Teams Work Best: 6,000 Team Members and Leaders Tell What It Takes to Succeed

*The*
# HUMANITARIAN
# LEADER *in Each of Us*

7 Choices That Shape a Socially Responsible Life

## Frank LaFasto

## Carl Larson

Los Angeles | London | New Delhi
Singapore | Washington DC

Los Angeles | London | New Delhi
Singapore | Washington DC

FOR INFORMATION:

SAGE Publications, Inc.
2455 Teller Road
Thousand Oaks, California 91320
E-mail: order@sagepub.com

SAGE Publications Ltd.
1 Oliver's Yard
55 City Road
London EC1Y 1SP
United Kingdom

SAGE Publications India Pvt. Ltd.
B 1/I 1 Mohan Cooperative Industrial Area
Mathura Road, New Delhi 110 044
India

SAGE Publications Asia-Pacific Pte. Ltd.
33 Pekin Street #02-01
Far East Square
Singapore 048763

Acquisitions Editor:   Lisa Cuevas Shaw
Editorial Assistant:   MaryAnn Vail
Production Editor:   Kelle Schillaci, Eric Garner
Copy Editor:   Trey Thoelcke
Typesetter:   C&M Digitals (P) Ltd.
Proofreader:   Susan Schon
Indexer:   Jean Casalegno
Cover Designer:   Gail Buschman
Marketing Manager:   Helen Salmon
Permissions Editor:   Karen Ehrmann

Cover photographs (clockwise from top left): Used by
permission and courtesy of Anoop Khurana, Dr. Irving
and Elvira Williams, V. Tony Hauser, and Hemera/
Thinkstock.

Printed in the United States of America

*Library of Congress Cataloging-in-Publication Data*

LaFasto, Frank

The humanitarian leader in each of us : 7 choices that
shape a socially responsible life / Frank LaFasto,
Carl Larson.

p. cm.
Includes bibliographical references and index.

ISBN 978-1-4129-9922-9 (pbk. : acid-free paper)

1. Leadership. 2. Social entrepreneurship. I. Larson,
Carl II. Title.

HD57.7.L34 2012
658.4′092—dc23          2011025881

11 12 13 14 15 10 9 8 7 6 5 4 3 2

*To Barbara,*
*whose work on behalf of those who*
*are hungry and homeless*
*exemplifies the spirit of this book.*


*To Kitty,*
*whose caring and commitment*
*bring hope*
*to young people facing difficult*
*choices.*

# Contents

# Preface

The idea for this book has been germinating throughout our working lives. One of us has had a long career in corporate America; the other in academia. Together, we have studied, consulted with, and written about some of the most successful organizations, teams, and leaders of the past 50 years.

As we worked on projects together and separately, we would occasionally meet leaders we found particularly intriguing. These people were unique in two respects. First, these leaders were unselfish, motivated by the needs of others, and dedicated to making the world a better place. They devoted time and energy to improving the lives of others, not as a byproduct of their job or hobby, but as a central focus, a defining characteristic. Second, these leaders were good at helping others. They were effective, successful, and impactful. They had the motivation and ability to make a positive difference in society.

We decided to study some of these remarkable people and find out how they came to be *humanitarian leaders*. We discovered that although they come from different nations, cultures, and even generations, they have a great deal in common. We are honored to share their stories, along with our insights, in this book.

*The Humanitarian Leader in Each of Us* is intended for college students and all those who aspire to a different kind of life—one that is, at the same time, socially responsible and personally fulfilling. We have included the following features that we hope will help you start or continue your own journey of helping others.

- Chapters 1 through 7 describe our discovery of an inner path of choices that led the people in this book to become humanitarian leaders.
- Chapters 8 and 9 look at humanitarian leadership through a wider lens, focusing on the impact of 31 people on urgent social problems, and the relationship between helping and personal happiness.
- Questions for discussion and individual reflection appear at the end of the first nine chapters.
- Chapter 10, the final chapter of the book, offers practical guidance and resources that can help you get started in a helping effort.

And now, we invite you to meet some very interesting people . . .

*Frank LaFasto*
*Carl Larson*

# Introduction

## The Moment

*The Same Look I Saw in the Mirror*

It was 5 o'clock one morning in 1994, and Susie Scott Krabacher couldn't sleep. Seated on the couch in her Aspen, Colorado, living room, she flipped through the television channels, hoping to find an episode of *Murder, She Wrote* that would take her mind off her problems. Susie's marriage to her attorney husband, who was asleep in the couple's bedroom, was in trouble. Her days had settled into a predictable pattern: trips to the gym, lunch with girlfriends, half-hearted attempts to run an antiques business. A former *Playboy* centerfold, Susie hadn't found a focus for her life since she left Hugh Hefner's mansion 10 years ago.

Suddenly, Susie's attention shifted to the documentary that was flickering across the screen. The topic was the terrible poverty in Ulan Bator, Mongolia, but what grabbed Susie's attention was the desolate look of a young boy glancing into the camera. Susie, a victim of repeated sexual abuse as a child, recognized the pain of this child who lived thousands of miles away; she had seen the same expression on her own face in the mirror as a young girl.

"When I was really little, I would sit on the vanity in the bathroom and look at myself in the mirror and cry and cry, and I just thought I looked so old. I used to think that I looked like the ladies at church that were really old. I thought that I had the same kind of eyes," Susie remembered. Deeply troubled, Susie lay awake, thinking about her own tortured childhood and the child on the television screen. As night gave way to day, she remembered a vow she had made as a little girl. "I started thinking, what if I did what I promised God that I'd do when I was little. I remembered during those little prayers when I mumbled constantly, if you let me survive I promise I will help other kids." By 7 a.m., Susie had a plan to do just that.

As it turned out, Susie's original plan to build an orphanage in Ulan Bator evolved into a larger humanitarian effort closer to home. A friend from church asked Susie why she was traveling "halfway around the world" to help children in Mongolia when Haiti, just 500 miles (805 kilometers) off the coast of Florida, had the poorest, most dangerous slums on the planet and was in desperate need of assistance. Susie was convinced, and that April she made her first trip to the island nation.

Nothing prepared her for the intense poverty and suffering that she witnessed in the Haitian capital of Port-au-Prince. "There is no sewage system in Haiti, none whatsoever," Susie explained. "All of the feces, the waste from the morgues, from the rich people's toilets, flows into the slum, Cité Soleil, and then out to the ocean." And when Susie made the bold decision to learn more about the living conditions by spending the night in Cité Soleil, which is rife with gang violence, she wasn't even sure if she would live to see the next morning.

But what ensured Susie's safety and made her trip life changing was the deep bond she developed with the Haitian people. "I didn't feel intimidated there," she said. "I felt like I was needed." Susie knew she had found her life's calling and soon found a building that she would turn into an orphanage. She eventually founded the Mercy & Sharing Foundation, a charity that operates schools and orphanages throughout Haiti and feeds and provides medical care to thousands of women and children. Following the devastating earthquake that struck on January 12, 2010, Susie worked tirelessly to locate all the children in her care, repair and reconstruct buildings, and reassemble her staff, which was scattered and traumatized after the disaster.

We asked ourselves why Susie Scott Krabacher and others like her stand up and say, "I am the one. It is my responsibility to help those in need," when so many others do not. We spent 5 years researching the answer to this question. Along the way, we met a remarkable group of leaders.

A nurse leaves her comfortable life in Hawaii to help educate and provide health care for vulnerable women and children in sub-Saharan Africa. A cancer surgeon travels to impoverished areas of Russia and Latvia with a team of volunteers to perform and teach lifesaving procedures. A man builds an orphanage in Tanzania where 290 of the 2,500 residents of a village are children who have lost both parents to AIDS. A college student with cystic fibrosis donates her time to teach English as a second language to adults. A young boy helps build more than 630 wells in 16 countries where water for drinking and farming is a precious commodity. A successful corporate attorney leaves a lucrative position to teach middle school students in inner-city Chicago. A U.S. soldier in Iraq organizes a massive effort to save the life of one local boy with a heart defect. A college graduate joins the Peace Corps. A priest gives 60 percent of his liver to a parishioner. A middle-class schoolteacher in India ignores the ridicule and warnings of her peers to found a network of train "platform schools" to educate the impoverished children who live in India's railway stations. The list goes on.

In this book, we explore 30 such stories of leadership for social good and identify the common attributes of those who are making a difference in the lives of others. Our intent was to learn from those who have had a significant impact, so that others might find a way to make a difference as well.[1]

## The Focus of This Book

For nearly a century, research on leadership has offered valuable insights, from the importance of individual traits and behavioral styles to the implications of the situations and contexts in which leaders find themselves. Most of the theories and models of leadership that have been developed describe what leadership looks like, how it might be conceptualized and understood, when it is full blown and functioning.[2]

What intrigued us about the leaders we studied was something different. We wanted to understand how they came to be leaders and, specifically, the kind of leaders who contribute to the well-being of people in need, and thereby to the larger human condition. Our objective was to trace the various leadership initiatives, actions, and choices back to their origins in the life of each leader.

We began with a simple assumption: *Life is preparation for leadership.* Or as Warren Bennis wrote in *On Becoming a Leader,* "the process of becoming a leader is much the same as the process of becoming an integrated human being. For the leader, as for any integrated person, life itself is the career."[3]

We have been studying leaders and other individuals with a bias toward action for nearly 40 years, but some fundamental questions remained unanswered: What causes some people to become interested enough in an issue to want to do something about it? What causes them to overcome the inertia of complacency and take the first small step? In short, how do they go from doing nothing to doing something?

As we thought about these questions, our focus became sharper. We asked ourselves, in the context of a society, why do some people assume ownership for helping those in need? Why are they willing to go it alone when no one is watching or applauding their efforts? Why are they willing to lead by personally doing, as well as by asking others to be involved?

In our search for answers, we chose to look at a group of highly effective individuals we call humanitarian leaders, *those who take charge of helping people in need.* They are empathic leaders who summon the personal initiative, energy, and effort necessary to improve the lives of others. Robert Greenleaf, who developed the concept of the servant leader in the early 1970s, placed a similar emphasis on the altruistic, empathic leader. Greenleaf's servant leader is highly focused on caring for and nurturing followers, but he or she also assumes responsibility for helping the less advantaged in society. Greenleaf wrote that "caring for persons, the more able and the less able serving each other, is the rock upon which a good society is built."[4]

In their composite portrait, our interviewees are a diverse group. They range in age from 16 to 88 years old. When they began their efforts to help others, one of them was only 6 years old and another only 7. Both men and women, they are multicultural in origin and even more so in focus. They are of different spiritual beliefs and religious backgrounds. Their educational levels range from middle school to doctorate level, and their incomes vary widely. Some have careers; some are retired. Their combined persona is a testament to the fact that leadership in society is defined by compassion, commitment, and character, not by calendars, cultures, or chromosomes.

Our intent in this book was not to present a general trait analysis of effective leaders. We leave that to the trait theorists, who have explored this approach since the early 1900s.[5] As we noted earlier, our interest was rather in understanding the journey our interviewees took to become the kind of leaders who help others. Nonetheless, as we talked with the leaders in this book, and in some cases observed them in action, we noticed a consistent contour to their personal qualities—qualities that we believe influenced their ability to make the leadership choices they did.

In their collective profile, our interviewees are modest, putting others at ease with their humility toward those they serve. They recognize there is unfairness in the world, but they focus on righting the imbalance. They need no encouragement to make a positive difference in the world. They are independent thinkers and self-empowered. They are street smart, bringing clear reasoning to a problem and uncompromising common sense: child prostitution is wrong, polio must be eradicated, starvation kills. They overcome apprehension by focusing on their goals, and they are resilient and resourceful in getting there. They don't get bitter about setbacks; instead, they are adaptable. They try again, differently, harder. They are prudent risk-takers. They come in from the circumference of a safe distance, roll up their sleeves, and get involved. They are hands-on. Their efforts are not in the abstract but in the practical and concrete. They are optimistic. They radiate enthusiasm and traffic in hope, looking forward, not back. They are self-sacrificing. They accept that making a difference comes with a price, but they are willing to pay it. They are each happy in their work and highly satisfied. They are each leading a larger life, as are those they help.

As we trace the footsteps of these leaders, we quickly realize there is no sanitized version of their stories. Children are victimized into prostitution and slave labor. There is parental suicide and murder. There are acts of generosity by soldiers in the midst of war. There are surgeries to correct facial deformities, and valiant attempts to uplift the spirits of children with serious ailments. The intimate realities of their stories are unknown by most, skirted by many.

While each person's story is absorbing, together they are instructive. Collectively, they bring more texture and depth to the picture of leadership for social good and demonstrate to the rest of us how we can share our time, energy, and talent to contribute to a better world. Their combined narrative shows us how we might evolve good intentions into good deeds.

## Our Research

Our aim in writing this book was not simply to recount the stories of individual leaders, as compelling as they are. Rather, we have sought to investigate the sources of humanitarian leadership in a way that can enable more of us to tap these wellsprings of social concern in ourselves.

Our research strategy was guided more by grounded theory than by any other approach.[6] Within grounded theory, we developed a sampling strategy in two phases. The first half of our sample, the first 15 interviews, came from a variety of contexts, from hurricanes to home-building, from organ donation to combat in war. Those cases were selected purposively to create divergence or differences in the sample. The second half of our sample, the final 15 interviews, was selected to create convergence or similarity in the sample, so that we could study more carefully the dominant themes that were emerging from the first 15 interviews. We selected cases that were characterized by longevity of impact, difficulty of the challenges, and involvement of others. For the second half of the sample, we were extremely fortunate to have had the cooperation of an international organization that satisfied the requirements for this phase of the research. This organization, World of Children, identifies, recognizes, and supports individuals who have made a significant difference in the quality of life for children around the world.

Our conversation with each of our interviewees had a twofold purpose. First, we wanted to better understand each person in terms of the life experiences that shaped who they are: their childhood background, the role models and people who influenced them, as well as events or experiences that helped define how they think, feel, and act in the context of their chosen role in society. Second, we wanted to learn more about their contributions to humanity: why they got involved and how they went about making a difference. Each assessment interview followed a consistent set of open-ended questions (see the appendix). We taped the interviews, transcribed the tapes, and analyzed the transcripts in order to find any recurring patterns, any qualities or properties that were present in every case. We wanted a composite description of these people that answers the question: What is unique about these people who help others? In the chapters that follow, we have narrowed our focus to include only those patterns that occur with greatest consistency.

## What We Discovered

From the responses of our interviewees, we discovered a path—a progression of sorts—that they moved along when taking responsibility for helping others. This path is marked by seven choice points. Each of these choices represents a willful act, one that involves making a clear and conscious decision to move toward making life better in some way for others.

The path of choices begins internally and reaches outward. Each of these choices represents a threshold that our leaders have passed through. In this sense, each threshold serves as a filter. Any of our interviewees might have dropped out at any point along the path. For example, one of our interviewees might have made a connection through personal experiences with a troubling social issue, such as homelessness, but then decided that it's just the way life is; everyone has to fend for themselves. That interviewee might never have moved any farther along the path. A choice could have been made to exit the path at any point.

**This is the path:**

1. **The leaders we interviewed leverage their life experiences.** This reflection on their own life stories—both positive and troubling—allows them to feel empathy for others and connect personally and deeply with their needs.

2. **They have a sense of fairness.** They understand that while life is not equally fair to everyone, a commitment to redressing inequities in society is everyone's responsibility.

3. **They believe they can matter.** Our interviewees avoid the rationalizations that might prevent them from helping and choose to believe they have what it takes to make a difference in the lives of others.

4. **They are open to an opportunity to help.** They are leaders with a positive mind-set that predisposes them to respond to people in need.

5. **They start by taking a small step.** They are realistic and practical in their expectations. And although the first step is small and its implications unknown, it is at this point that leadership begins to emerge.

6. **They persevere.** They are leaders who are not easily discouraged in the face of often daunting obstacles because their goals are important to them.

7. **They lead the way.** They build a collective energy and enthusiasm for an effort or cause, thereby encouraging others to share the passion and become involved.

This book describes how our leaders made their choices to contribute in ways both large and small to the well-being of society. We believe that by understanding the path they followed, it is possible to gain the confidence and self-knowledge that can shorten the distance between wanting to help others and taking meaningful action.

Perhaps you will find yourself somewhere along the path and discover a way to take the next step as part of your own journey of leadership for social good. As our interviewees have demonstrated, humanitarian leadership is a choice, and it's one that is accessible to anyone who is committed to promoting the welfare of others.  Rather than being difficult to grasp and to do well except by certain extraordinary individuals or those in positions of power, humanitarian leadership is within the reach of anyone with the drive and desire to make the world a better place. Certainly, people can become more effective leaders by understanding leadership theory and practice, but as we have observed, leadership that is fueled by a desire to help others emerges in a surprisingly uncomplicated way.

Finally, it's important to keep in mind that the context in which you contribute is not what matters most, for worthy goals are everywhere—in the workplace, community, places of worship, and the larger world in which we live. Nor does it matter whether you volunteer a few hours a week in your own community or devote your professional career to helping others. What does matter is summoning sufficient initiative, energy, and commitment to make something worthwhile happen—in short, to make a difference.

---

Here we introduce you to the 31 humanitarian leaders:

**Dr. Jane Aronson:** pediatrician in New York City and founder of the Worldwide Orphans Foundation, dedicated to enhancing the lives of children in orphanages around the world

**Jennifer Atler:** former corporate attorney and past executive director of Invest in Kids, a Colorado-based program that works to improve the health and well-being of children

**Larry Bradley:** U.S. Army Major in Iraq who spearheaded an effort, while on active duty, to save the life of a seriously ill Iraqi boy

**Meg Campbell:** founder of Codman Academy Charter Public School in Dorchester, Massachusetts, an innovative school for students of color and from low-income and single-parent households

**Hui-jung Chi:** former journalist, now CEO of the Garden of Hope Foundation, dedicated to creating a gender equal society and improving the lives of disadvantaged women and girls in Taiwan

**Liz Clibourne ("Mama Liz"):** nurse and teacher from Hawaii who volunteers in Africa with a special interest in children affected by HIV/AIDS, as well as an interest in women's health issues; founder of Every Child Every Village, an organization that created "teaching without books," a successful, inexpensive approach that involves painting lessons on preschool classroom walls

**Victor Dukay:** entrepreneur from Denver, Colorado, and AIDS community leader in Tanzania; through the Lundy Foundation, built an orphanage for children who have lost parents to AIDS and supports Test & Treat to End AIDS, an international effort to eliminate the disease by stopping its transmission

**Kathryn Funderburk:** longtime volunteer despite her own battle with cystic fibrosis and diabetes; Harvard University graduate who, as a student, led diabetes organizations on campus and in the neighboring community; now a teacher at City on a Hill Charter Public School in the Roxbury neighborhood of Boston

**Kathy Giusti:** founder and CEO of the Multiple Myeloma Research Foundation in Norwalk, Connecticut, which funds research into new drugs and fosters collaboration in the myeloma research community; honored by *Time* magazine as one of the 100 most influential people of 2011

**Mike and Tracey Goffman:** contractors in Bristol, Wisconsin, who took in a family whose home was lost in Hurricane Katrina and provided aid to other displaced residents

**Father Gary Graf:** former pastor in Waukegan, Illinois, and liver donor to a parishioner; now pastor of St. Gaal Church in Chicago

**Lucy Helm:** deputy general counsel at Starbucks Coffee Company and codirector of Camp Parkview, a residential camp for developmentally challenged adults in Washington state

**Ryan Hreljac:** founder, at age 9, of Ryan's Well Foundation in Ontario, Canada, which has raised more than $2 million for water and sanitation projects on three continents

**Inderjit Khurana:** teacher and founder of network of train "platform schools," which educate thousands of street children in Bhubaneswar, India; Inderjit passed away at age 74 in 2010

**Craig Kielburger:** Canadian children's rights activist and founder, at age 12, of Free The Children, the world's largest network of young people helping other young people through education

**Sherri Kirkpatrick:** a nurse who has worked with health workers and vulnerable children in developing countries for more than 25 years; cofounded HealthEd Connect, a nonprofit with a mission to empower women and children through evidence-based health, education, and advocacy programs

**Sanphasit Koompraphant:** founder of the Center for the Protection of Children's Rights in Thailand, which works to protect abused and neglected children and prevent child trafficking and other exploitative practices; advocate for child protection legislation; past president of the International Society for the Prevention of Child Abuse and Neglect

**Susie Scott Krabacher:** founder of the Mercy & Sharing Foundation of Aspen, Colorado, which works to improve the health and quality of life for women and children in Haiti

**Harry Leibowitz:** former business executive and founder of World of Children, a California-based organization that honors people who have made outstanding contributions to the well-being of children around the world

**Kathy Magee:** founder, with her plastic surgeon husband, of Operation Smile, a Norfolk, Virginia-based organization that has provided more than 160,000 surgeries for children with facial deformities around the world

**Cheryl Perera:** founder, at age 19, of the Canada-based OneChild Network, a youth-led organization with a mission to end the global commercial sexual exploitation of children

**Peter Samuelson:** media executive, movie producer, and founder of the Starlight Children's Foundation in Los Angeles, which offers educational and recreational services to seriously ill children internationally; First Star, which advocates for foster children nationally; and Everyone Deserves a Roof (EDAR), which provides mobile housing for the homeless

**William Sergeant:** head of the Rotary International PolioPlus Committee for more than 12 years; full-time volunteer based in Knoxville, Tennessee, working toward worldwide eradication of polio; passed away at age 91 in 2011 and was recognized posthumously with the Rotary International PolioPlus Committee Champion Award

**Gerry Sieck:** former corporate attorney who became a middle school teacher in inner-city Chicago

**Makenzie Snyder:** founder, at age 8, of Children to Children, an all-volunteer program in Bowie, Maryland, that provides foster children with duffel bags in which to carry their belongings with dignity as they move from home to home

**Rob Taylor:** firefighter and paramedic in Puyallup, Washington, who has traveled to Mexico to build affordable houses for needy families

**Dave Ulrich:** professor at the Ross School of Business of the University of Michigan and missionary leader in Quebec who provided counseling and educational services to local residents

**Margaret Vernon:** Peace Corps volunteer from Colorado, specializing in public health in Burkina Faso; also helped create microcredit groups for local women; now living and working in Rwanda

**Dr. Irving Williams:** pediatrician from Rockville, Maryland, and founder, along with his wife, Elvira, of Adventures in Health, Education & Agricultural Development, which has worked for more than 30 years to reduce and eliminate disease and premature death in Tanzania, The Gambia, and the United States

**Dr. David J. Winchester:** surgical oncologist in Evanston, Illinois, and member of volunteer medical team, Bridges Across the Atlantic, that has brought lifesaving surgery and medical training to Russia, Latvia, and more recently, China

# Part One

## Making a Connection

*Mtu ni watu*

(*A person is people.*)

—*Swahili proverb*

# 1

# Leveraging Life's Experiences

## *A Generation of Orphans*

V ictor Dukay was 15 years old and away at boarding school when his life fell apart in its entirety. It wasn't because of anything that happened at school, but rather what happened at home.

On the morning of November 5, 1971, Victor's father, a psychiatrist who had been suffering from clinical depression, came down to the breakfast table with a revolver in his hand. With unexplainable and systematic disregard, according to Victor, he shot and killed his wife and his daughter. He took two shots at Victor's brother, missed, and then shot himself. A double murder suicide.

For Victor, at the un-adult age of 15, it became the defining moment of his life. Instantly, Victor was unmoored and lost. He was horrified with the present and suspicious of any promise of future happiness. With despair looming large, Victor made an agreement with himself that involved the possibility of ending his own life.

"I made a pact with myself," Victor remembered. "By the age of 40, if I actually felt the way I felt after losing my parents, I would kill myself. That was what actually allowed me, at the darkest moments, to know that if it continued as painfully as it was, I would have an out."

This radical ultimatum forced Victor to search for some sense of meaning to his life. For some time, he found none. His teens and twenties were spent in high school, in college, and acquiring a master's degree in business. After graduate school, with experience flying planes since he was 17, Victor started an executive jet business and made money. He then sold his business and went back to graduate school again, this time for a doctorate in human communication.

But through all of the searching, a meaningfulness to his life was nowhere to be found. Then Victor and a friend named Steve Lundy, whom he had met through church, began volunteering at Mother Teresa's Hospice in Denver, Colorado. When meaning finally did arrive, it arrived unannounced, and with existential weight.

"I started to make the connection at Hospice," Victor told us. "That's where I actually had enough time to feel. Up to that point, I was disconnected with heart and brain because I was so tired and emotionally exhausted. When I actually had time to be connected and to feel once again, that's when the path became clear as to what I should be doing. Not exactly the path, or exactly the feeling, but that I should be doing something that involved service."[1]

Sadly, not long after Victor and Steve began volunteering at the hospice, Steve revealed that he was HIV positive. "At that point in the journey, drugs had not yet been developed," Victor explained. "I became his caretaker and caregiver, and we developed an intimate friendship as he was dying. Steve told me he wanted to leave some money to make a difference. I told him I had just sold a company. We each put in $100,000 and created the Lundy Foundation."

The Lundy Foundation was established as a public operating charity in 1991. Today, the foundation is active in HIV/AIDS-related issues, most notably a major project to eradicate the deadly pandemic through regular HIV testing, followed by immediate antiretroviral treatment for those who test positive. The foundation is also an active participant in an international initiative to assess the effectiveness of AIDS programs that target orphaned and vulnerable children in East Africa.

Why Africa? Because, Victor said, he had come to the painful realization that the AIDS epidemic in Africa would create an entire generation of orphans, just like himself. "I am an orphan. I will always be orphaned," Victor told us. "No matter how much money I have or how many friends I have, I will always be orphaned. There is a piece of me that I lost at an early age. That's what I get connected to when I am in Africa."

Victor pointed out that the terrible tragedy that happened to him has paradoxically had the very positive effect of motivating him to do the work he is doing in Africa with kids. "There were people when my parents and sister died who took me in and decided they were going to help this one lonely soul," Victor said. "I think I am doing the same thing with my life right now. I am trying to help the 60 kids that I can and hopefully make a difference in their lives because somebody helped me. I know what it feels like at a very deep level of having somebody reach their arm out and say, 'Come with us.'"

For Victor, life became more meaningful while he was caring for a dying friend. Through his friendship with Steve Lundy, a compassion emerged for those who are alone—whether living or dying. "I reached 40, and it seemed that not all of the pain goes away, because it never does, but I responded to it differently," Victor said. "I know at some level, not exactly, but at some level, what those kids are feeling and I can help somehow or another."

Although profoundly moving, the way in which Victor made a deep emotional connection with the AIDS orphans of Africa is not unusual among our interviewees. In fact, making an empathic connection[2] is the first of seven choices we observed among those we interviewed. We'll look at the other six choices in the following chapters of this book.

## Empathic Connections

Like Victor, all of our interviewees allowed us passage into their inner circle of one, where they gave us a detailed reflection of their own lives. Good leadership begins with self-awareness. Proponents of the *authentic leadership* approach contend such self-awareness is rooted in an understanding of the larger meaning of the stories leaders tell about themselves.[3] Indeed, as our interviewees narrated their life stories, they described personal experiences and connections they said deepened their desire to help others.

These emotional connections have drawn the attention of other researchers as well, and there is now increasing interest in understanding the kinds of connections people make with one another, as well as their biological basis.[4] A remarkable groundbreaking discovery called *mirror neurons*,[5] for example, has prompted a new interdisciplinary field, social neuroscience, to investigate empathic connections. Using brain imaging and other leading-edge technologies that allow scientists to peer inside the human brain, researchers have discovered that we can mirror another person's neural activities and "share" pain, disgust, taste, smell, and other feelings and sensations.[6] We have observed a heightened capacity in our interviewees to "share" the internal states of others.[7]

In fact, all of the leaders we interviewed for this book have demonstrated a compassion and empathy for the people they serve that is immediately obvious.[8] What's not so obvious are the reasons behind this strong underlying presence of empathy. What we discovered in the course of our interviews is that in each case, their compassion and desire to help are in some way leveraged by a personal experience, often occurring in childhood, that imprinted them with an understanding and appreciation for how another person might feel when challenged by one of life's circumstances. As we learned, their empathy has its early roots in one or more of three sources: exposure to role models and positive values, experiencing a troubling awareness, or having a traumatic personal experience.

## Role Models and Positive Values

Many of our interviewees told us that positive experiences they had early in their lives created a lasting impression about the importance of social responsibility. Not surprisingly, these experiences often included an altruistic role model. That role model was most often a mother, father, or other family member, who passed on their own values of serving others.[9] But a role model need not be a family member. It also can be a teacher, community worker, religious leader, or even a friend. Leadership researchers Kouzes and Posner underscore the power of "modeling the way" as a means of transmitting a set of values to others. They write that we trust leaders—or, in this case, parents, teachers, and other role models—when their "deeds and words match."[10]

In 2001, Meg Campbell founded Codman Academy Charter Public School in Dorchester, Massachusetts, a high school that has had tremendous success in preparing students from disadvantaged families for admission to 4-year colleges. A graduate of Radcliffe College (now part of Harvard), Meg had her choice of prestigious, well-paying jobs after graduation. But Meg had clearly been influenced by her large, socially committed family. Her mother was a history teacher, whom Meg modeled herself after, even as a little girl. "I was always playing school," she told us. "There's something kind of magical for me about schools."

Another important role model for Meg was Anne Sullivan, the gifted teacher who led a young Helen Keller out of her closed world of darkness and silence. Meg told us that reading about Sullivan influenced her choice of Radcliffe, which the renowned teacher had attended. She also said that she identified with the young and inexperienced Sullivan, who faced the daunting challenge of reaching a blind and deaf girl, but who told herself, "I'm the best one here; I'm the only one here." Herself undaunted by those who said high school was too late to change young people's lives, Meg succeeded in starting a secondary school that sought to shape students' characters, as well as advance their academic prospects, thus setting them on the path to a better life.

Other people we talked with were similarly influenced by positive role models. Margaret Vernon joined the Peace Corps right after her graduation from Georgetown University. She told us her decision was influenced by her father, who is a general surgeon, and her mother, who works in international health. Together, Margaret's parents reinforced the importance of taking responsibility for improving health care for people in developing parts of the world. Margaret, who at the time of our interview was a public health volunteer in West Africa, said, "A large part of what I am doing now is probably due to their teachings and what they showed me as I was growing up."

Dave Ulrich spent 3 years with his wife in Quebec leading missionaries for his church. To do so required Dave to take a sabbatical from his professorship at the University of Michigan, as well as leave behind a lucrative consulting practice. Dave told us his decision was strongly influenced by his experience as a child helping his father make chili every Sunday and then taking it to a local homeless shelter. "When our family talks about service, there are no ifs, ands, or buts," Dave said. "You give back."

Harry Leibowitz is the founder of World of Children, an organization that honors individuals who make a difference in the lives of children around the globe. Even though Harry grew up poor as the son of immigrants in Brooklyn, New York, he told us he learned the beginnings of social responsibility from his grandmother, who taught him to follow the Jewish tradition of giving some of his few coins to Israel. Although she was "an old-world person" who didn't speak English very well, Harry's grandmother was "really critical in my understanding of and appreciation of people," Harry told us.

Peter Samuelson is the founder of the Starlight Children's Foundation, which helps seriously ill children and their families cope. Peter told us he was strongly influenced by his high-achieving and philanthropically engaged father, "who cast a very long shadow." Born in London, Peter came to Los Angeles after university to begin his career as a motion picture and television producer, but he said, "We carry the legacy of our parents with us." For Peter, that legacy bore fruit in his own now wide-reaching philanthropic ventures.

Dr. Irving Williams is the founder of Adventures in Health, Education & Agricultural Development. Irving remembers his father, a farmer, telling him as a boy, "We must grow more things than we think we will need for ourselves. Grow some things for the birds and animals to eat. Grow some things to give to other people." Irving has followed the spirit of this advice, devoting his life to improving the health and well-being of people in developing countries, where children often suffer from malaria, polio, diarrhea, and other preventable diseases. Through his efforts in rural African communities for the past 26 years, thousands of children's lives have been saved. Moreover, Irving has taught doctors, nurses, and other health care specialists how to grow high-quality, nutrient-rich foods, thereby sharing the knowledge and skills he learned as a boy growing up on his family farm.

While many of our interviewees were inspired to help others by the example of role models, nearly all also pointed to their faith as a guiding force that shaped their values about service. Perhaps most strikingly, Father Gary Graf, a priest in Waukegan, Illinois, offered to give 60 percent of his liver to a parishioner he barely knew, a man named Miguel Zavala, who would have otherwise died. Reflecting back, Father Gary places the decision in the context of his spiritual life, noting that donating part of his liver "seems to make sense in the larger context of who I am and what I would do and should do."

Of course, one doesn't have to be a priest or other religious leader to be guided by faith. Dr. Jane Aronson, the founder of Worldwide Orphans Foundation, grew up in a Reform Jewish family and describes herself as "traditionally and spiritually a Jewish person." She told us that she follows the Jewish teaching of *tikkun olam,* or repairing the world, which she described as "a very old Hebrew concept that is embedded in the thousands of years of Jewish life and which means that we are put in this world to be committed to justice in the world." Jane, a pediatrician, has made that concept a reality in her life's work. Through her foundation, she has helped better the lives of more than 5,000 children around the world who are orphans or who live without consistent parental care.

Hui-jung Chi of Taiwan also has been guided and sustained by her Christian faith, which she describes as her core value. Like many of the people we interviewed, Hui-jung experienced an intersection of positive role models and faith; she was inspired to attend Sunday school and learn the Bible by her devout Christian parents. A former journalist, Hui-jung has been an important voice against child prostitution, domestic violence, and sexual abuse. Hui-jung revitalized the Garden of Hope Foundation, now a network of counseling centers, emergency shelters, and long-term halfway houses for girls rescued from forced prostitution or otherwise in need. Her work has benefited more than 150,000 children in Taiwan, but fighting for the rights of abused children in a country where the government has long ignored the problem and where children have been seen traditionally as property has taken great courage, perseverance, and skill. "I can get through anything with the help of God," Hui-jung told us.

## A Troubling Awareness

While for some of our interviewees empathy was nurtured by role models and positive values and experiences, other interviewees described their deep connection as the result of a troubling awareness about some aspect of society. Once again, we observed a consistent pattern.

Consider how a sudden awareness of reality resonated deeply with the following interviewees. In each case, the awareness ignited a passion to do something to help that could hardly have been arrived at by chance alone.

Makenzie Snyder, the young founder of Children to Children, was only 7 years old when she attended a Children's World Summit meeting with her two brothers and met foster care children for the first time. Makenzie, 16 at the time of our interview, said she was "appalled" to discover that many foster children are forced to take their belongings with them in plastic trash bags as they move from home to home, an indignity that compounds the already harrowing situation for a youngster of being separated from parents and siblings. The kids Makenzie met told her they had been in as many as 13 different homes.

"I felt sympathy for them," Makenzie said, "and I knew what they were going through in a way, like I understood." She found what she had learned from the foster care children so disturbing that she convinced her parents to go with her to yard sales to collect duffel bags and stuffed animals that she could donate to foster children. Shortly thereafter, she began collecting donations from businesses, including Freddie Mac, and individuals alike. To date, Makenzie has handed out more than 60,000 duffel bags, each containing a small stuffed animal, to foster children. "When I'm upset, I like to have a stuffed animal to cuddle with," Makenzie confided, demonstrating the compassion she has for youngsters in less fortunate circumstances than her own.

Craig Kielburger, at the age of 12, founded Free The Children to fight oppressive child labor practices. While looking for the comics section in the newspaper, Craig came across a story of a young Pakistani boy, a boy his same age, who was murdered for speaking out against child labor. Craig was so upset by this blunt awareness that he stood in front of his classmates and asked for their help. He formed a group of 12 students that began raising money, awareness, and petitioning against forced child labor.

Ryan Hreljac, at the age of 9, founded Ryan's Well Foundation, which has helped build more than 630 wells and other water projects in 16 countries. Ryan was moved when his first grade teacher explained to the class that many people in the world were dying because they didn't have access to clean water. "When I was 6 years old, I guess I was pretty naïve, and I thought there were two towns in the world, and our town had water and another one didn't, and one well would fix it," Ryan explained. "Now, you grow up and you learn there are a billion people in the world who don't have clean water, and every 8 seconds another child dies."

Cheryl Perera is the founder of OneChild Network, dedicated to eliminating the commercial sexual exploitation of children. At the age of 16, Cheryl was enraged to learn that Sri Lanka, the land of her own heritage, was a perilous trap for nearly 40,000 children forced or conned into prostitution. Cheryl was so disturbed by these statistics that she took several months off from high school to investigate child prostitution in Sri Lanka. She even played the main role in a treacherous undercover sting operation that removed a dangerous pedophile from the streets. During the sting, Cheryl connected in a profound way with the horror of what she was witnessing. "For that little while," she told us, "I understood what it was to have my childhood seen as a commodity."

Jennifer Atler, a former corporate attorney, is the past executive director of Invest in Kids, an evidence-based community program dedicated to improving the health and well-being of children from low-income families. Jennifer was inspired by the courage of her mother, a former Miss America, after a newspaper reporter identified her as a child victim of sexual abuse, and the story became front-page news. Jennifer told us that after the revelation, which was met with shock and disbelief in their community, her mother held a meeting at their church that was attended by more than 1,100 people. The meeting became a pivotal moment in Jennifer's life. From then on, she told us, she knew she wanted to work with children, so that others would not have to endure what her mother had experienced.

## A Traumatic Personal Experience

Not unlike Victor Dukay, whose life was shaped by losing both of his parents and sister at an early age, several other interviewees reported experiences that were, in their own way, challenging enough to shape their empathy and fuel their desire to help others.[11]

Kathy Giusti, along with her twin sister, Karen, established the Multiple Myeloma Research Foundation (MMRF) in 1998 soon after Kathy received the devastating diagnosis of multiple myeloma, an incurable cancer of the blood. The 5-year survival rate is one of the lowest of all cancers. Nearly 20,000 adults are diagnosed with multiple myeloma in the United States every year, and 11,000 people are predicted to die from the illness. But Kathy, a mother of two who has now had the disease for 15 years, is a fighter.

Kathy was determined to apply the management skills she had learned as a successful corporate executive to battling the disease. As the world's number-one private sponsor of multiple myeloma research, the MMRF, which facilitates collaboration among researchers, funds nearly 120 laboratories worldwide. The results have been significant. Today, the MMRF supports 70 new compounds and approaches in clinical trials that are extending and improving the lives of patients until a cure can be found.

We have already met Susie Scott Krabacher in this book's introduction. She's the founder of Mercy & Sharing Foundation, which feeds and provides health care to abandoned children in the desperate slum of Cité Soleil in Haiti. Susie, you will recall, told us that her desire to help children grew out of her own experience growing up in a physically and emotionally abusive family. When she saw an impoverished Mongolian boy on television one night, she identified with the look of despair on his face, a connection that spurred her to take actions that eventually led her to help the children of Haiti.

While a deep connection between a need they saw in society and their own experiences was made in many different ways, each interviewee made one. The connection between their inner reflection and the outer world became an inflection point in their lives. In the case of role models and positive values, the connection represents continuity from the lessons learned by the examples of others to becoming an example themselves. It required accepting a passing of the torch and assuming personal responsibility. Someone showed them how to serve society by serving the needs of others. Our interviewees have simply completed the loop.

Completing the cycle of learning is also true for those interviewees who experienced a troubling awareness: there are child slave laborers; some people have to travel long distances for a drink of water; foster children often carry their belongings in a trash bag; or discovering one's mother, a former Miss America, was sexually abused as a child. In each case they were required to answer a few simple questions. What should I do about this new awareness? Should I do something or should I do nothing? Making a personal connection with such troubling aspects of humanity required our interviewees to face a stark reality, one that left them exposed, looking eye to eye with their own values, asking themselves, "Knowing what I now know, what do I do?"

It's an even harsher reality for those interviewees who were subjected to a more personal trauma, such as Victor Dukay, Susie Krabacher, and Kathy Giusti. It's easy for us to imagine how their experiences could have resulted in an inward focus and even a negative outcome. Victor could have decided to take his own life at the age of 40. Susie could have become abusive to others, mirroring her own upbringing. Kathy Giusti could have attended privately to her own cancer and her family's needs.

But in each case, the opposite occurred. Our interviewees rebuilt, and even resculpted, their lives beyond the disappointment into something more. They did not indulge feelings unhinged by anger, but instead reconciled their feelings into a positive purpose. They found the motivation to transform their trauma into a meaningful mantra: orphans must not be alone, children must not live in terrible poverty, a deadly cancer must be cured.

It's about alternative lives sourced from the same experience. Somehow, they came to understand that they were free to choose how they played it out, positively or negatively, and they chose the positive. In short, they made the absolute best of a bad experience. It's what the renowned Viennese psychiatrist Viktor Frankl, who spent 3 years in the concentration camps of World War II, termed "tragic optimism."[12] It is human potential at its best, turning suffering into human achievement, changing oneself for the better and taking responsible action.

Deep connections begin with what we know. Whether encouraged by a positive virtue of a childhood role model or self-coaxed out of despair, our interviewees are deeply familiar with feelings that resonate in sharp, clear images. The faithful acknowledgment of their own experiences is liberating. They don't ignore the values they were taught, the insights they came across, or the trauma they experienced. They embrace them and focus on the need. They don't look for someone who is worthy of their time or generosity. They know the need itself is worthwhile: hunger, shelter, water, safety, and so on all stand on their own importance.

When he turned 40, Victor Dukay was still absorbing the impact of having been made what he calls an "instant orphan" at a young age. Somehow he found a way to reassemble his fractured youth into a higher purpose. He saw a connection between his life experiences and some deep cut in humanity. He knew with AIDS a generation of orphans would emerge. Victor Dukay rose to the occasion. Perhaps the poet Kahlil Gibran understood best the nature of our deepest connections when he wrote: "Out of suffering have emerged the strongest souls; the most massive characters are seared with scars."

Empathy is a feeling with its own temperament. Some needs resonate with us; others do not. The reasons are more unknown than known. The lesson from our interviewees is to begin with what we know about ourselves as a way to connect with our interest in helping others. Not everyone can work with the elderly, or spend time with a child who is dying, or look into the eyes of the homeless. But the lesson from our interviewees is that everyone can do something. It all begins by connecting with your passion and what matters to you.

As we saw in this chapter, the important first choice along the path is asking oneself, what is important to me, what do I connect with. The second choice, explored in the next chapter, leads to putting a stake in the ground about fairness in the world. This choice involves asking oneself whether people get what they deserve or are simply victims of ill fate.

## Finding Your Connection

If you have a desire to help others, but have yet to make a connection with what is really important to you, there is an uncomplicated way to proceed. Consider the following three-step process.

1. Think about your own life. Is there an experience that has left a particularly strong impression on you? What is it that you understand so well and feel so strongly about that you know the details of someone else's feelings on the same issue? Such topics as divorce, cancer, unemployment, child abuse, hunger, feeling marginalized, or being alone are just a few examples. As you make your connection, were you influenced by a positive role model in your life or by a personal experience or troubling awareness?

2. Ponder and reflect. When you think about the issue with which you are familiar, what feelings emerge? What do you know about other people who experience those feelings? What do you imagine they might be going through? What would you hope for them?

3. Consider your options. Do you feel strongly enough about the issue to want to help someone else through it? Do you feel a sense of responsibility to use your knowledge for the benefit of others? What if you do nothing? Would your lack of action have any implications for others? For you?

# 2

# A Sense of Fairness

*Bags of Magic*

The children inside the gate laughed, sang songs, and played with a ball. The children outside the gate watched them.

The 20 or so children outside the gate were different, a subset of the society in which they lived. They were children whose formative growth years would be stunted by their immediate world, one seemingly accustomed to disadvantage and disregard.

To Inderjit Khurana, the only teacher at her small school, there could be no starker contrast. As her surname reflects, Inderjit Khurana's cultural origin is India. The town where she began her school is Bhubaneswar. The year was 1978.

"The scene at my school used to be a few children inside the school and tons of children outside the entrance gate," Inderjit told us. "They came from neighboring slums. The children outside the gate would be naked or semiclad. They were disheveled and dirty because the parents were not at home. The parents were at work. Most of the girl children were carrying their little siblings around with them. An older girl wearing just a pair of panties carried a baby that was naked. The girl may have been 8 or 9 years old, and the baby was about 9 months.

"They were at the gate because they saw such fun and joy," Inderjit continued. "They didn't have a childhood like that. They were just left with duties, chores to be done at home such as look after the baby and cook the rice. They had very sad accidents because they were little children given a big responsibility. One of the young girls who was going to remove the water from the rice once it was done was pouring it out and the whole pan fell on her. Her left arm was completely burned."

The parents, Inderjit told us, put a cow dung plaster on the child's arm instead of informing anyone or taking her to the hospital. "It was only when we didn't see the girl outside the gate for about 10 days that we went to her home and found what had happened to her," Inderjit remembered. "She was lying on the bed with an infected wound. We treated her and got her to a hospital, but some of the skin had shrunk, and her arm couldn't be straightened. But at least her infection was gone."

These were the forgotten children of India, invisible to the middle-class world of Inderjit's students and their parents. But to Inderjit, their presence was conspicuous and troubling. She saw them congregate at the school gate each day; she saw them stare at her students with a mixture of wonder, confusion, and wistfulness; and she knew it was not right that while the children inside the gates went to school, those outside did not.

Inderjit wanted to do something for these children who she knew could never escape their impoverished lives without an education, but she realized there were powerful social barriers to overcome. If she let the poor children outside the gate come to the school free of charge, she told us, the middle-class parents would withdraw their children. "Either way it would fail, whatever I was doing," she said. Little did Inderjit know that she would find a way to turn this "lose-lose situation," as she called it, into a win-win.

Inderjit stood only 5 feet (1.5 meters) tall, but she always had lofty ambitions. She married young at age 19 and later earned her master's degree in history and received her teacher's training in early childhood education. In 1977 her husband retired, and they moved to Bhubaneswar, a city in the state of Orissa on the east coast of India. For the first 3 months, Inderjit was at a loss trying to settle into this new society. "Playing cards and partying were not something I wanted to do," she said. "That's what the other females did in that society. I wanted to be usefully occupied."

So she started a preschool center with just two 3-year-olds and no advertising. "I had just a little board to say it was *Ruchika,* which means something that is interesting and aesthetic. At the end of the year, I had 11 children. It was just by word of mouth. I was the only teacher, and I was also the only chauffeur. I was driving the children around in my car to see places of interest and taking them to the zoo and things like that. I think the visibility got the other nine children. I charged 40 rupees, or $1.00, for each child per month." The school's reputation steadily grew, and 7 years after it opened, enrollment had climbed to 90 students.

Despite the success of her school, Inderjit could not forget the children outside the gate. She recalled, in particular, how they seemed to mirror every move the Ruchika children made. "They smiled at the children when they were smiling. When the children were playing games and laughing, they would also laugh a little. I'm sure it crossed their minds, why couldn't they go to a place like the children inside the gate?" But Inderjit knew that there would never be a time when these children would be included in any learning environment like her school. She knew the sad truth, a destiny the children were too young to fully appreciate. Their time would never come.

After much deliberation, Inderjit came to an important realization. "I made a silent commitment that one day I would reach out to these children in a place where they would be accepted and where I could take the school to them. That's where the idea began: If the child cannot come to a school, then take the school to the child. I had to scout around before I chose the group which I found was the most appropriate. I found that group at the railway station."

Selecting her newest group of students at the railway station was no accident. Inderjit often found herself there, as the railway station is a major hub of activity in Bhubaneswar. She would see children wiping the trains' compartment floors and begging for money from passengers. Later on, Inderjit would discover that these "railway children" belonged to a vast underclass of millions of young people who lived in the streets. But in the beginning, all she cared about was helping these children who spent their days at the railway station, but who had no destination.

On April 7, 1985, confronted by long, hard odds, Inderjit took the first step toward helping the railway children. "I went to the railway station with a colleague of mine, and we just carried what we called our bags of magic," she remembered. "We each carried a bag of storybooks, crayons, paper, paints, some sweets for the end of class, and soap because I knew they would love a bath. As it turned out, the bath was the most popular activity. The children at the railway station, with the steam engines and sleeping on the floor, were always dirty. I thought, if their clothes were dirty at least their bodies should not have body lice, skin infections, and things like that." Inderjit and her fellow teacher had 11 children on the first day they went to the railway station. By November 12 of the same year, that number had reached 114.

Everyone, however, did not view the railway children with the same compassion that Inderjit showed. "From the beginning, we had a lot of train passengers coming in and saying, 'Why are you trying to educate these children? You think you are saving their lives? God has sent them into families like this because it was predestined. They were supposed to be poor, and they will remain poor, and they will remain uneducated. It is karma. They are paying for the karma of the last life by having a difficult time in this life.'"

Inderjit felt differently. In her eyes, they were simply children at the edge of humanity and in danger of falling off. "We had girls getting pregnant at age 12," Inderjit told us. "While promoting HIV/AIDS awareness, I would say to them, 'Do you know how sick you can get with this kind of open sex? You might just die!' This one young girl turned around and told me, 'But I'm dead already.' It's because she had no control over her body. It just earned her money to live."

Inderjit knew their troubles could not be washed away with a bar of soap. She also knew she did not want to merely nurture their status in life, but help them rise above it. After all, she believed, living in unlivable conditions is dehumanizing. Not having a way out is immoral. For them to find a better place in the world, Inderjit knew they must be educated. And she knew even a little education would go a long way toward avoiding a lifetime of humiliation.

Inderjit was the architect and driving force behind a simple but powerful improvement to her society: Take the school to the children.

From just one school, the Ruchika Social Service Organization has grown to include 17 platform schools at railway stations dotted across well over 100 miles (160 kilometers) of train track. The schools reach more than 500 children every day from the villages and cities along the trains' paths. "We don't deny admission to any child at the railway station," Inderjit explained. "They can come for a day, they can come for 2 days. We don't put rules on them. We put a child on the rules after he has been attending school somewhat regularly for 3 months. Then we know we have hope of transferring him to a formal school. About 50 children get mainstreamed to a regular school each year."

Inderjit eventually expanded her core philosophy of taking the school to the children with more than 100 centers of education, consisting of preschools and primary schools, for children in the slums. There is also a Toy Library on Wheels program with books and toys for children to enjoy. The need is great and growing. According to Inderjit, in Bhubaneswar alone, some 20,000 children don't go to school.

Inderjit Khurana's Ruchika movement does not answer the problems of poverty for every street child in India, or even for every deprived child in Bhubaneswar, but for those that it does help, it is a solution. In Inderjit's eyes, safety, education, and a happy childhood were not a fringe benefit available just to the privileged. For her, they were a dead center birthright. "If a child is happy and confident, that's all that is needed in life," Inderjit said. "The rest will follow."

At the end of our interview, Inderjit expressed her attitude toward fairness simply but eloquently, "I felt the haves and the have-nots marking in society was some taboo we had to break." If only by a small margin, she narrowed the gap. Inderjit's footprint may have been small, but it offered a huge stride toward a more positive future.

As we learned in Chapter 1, the people in this book have made a strong connection with others that is deeply rooted in empathy. A perception that there is some sort of injustice, or lack of fairness, at work profoundly intensifies that connection and is a powerful motivator to take action to right the wrong.[1] In fact, in philosophical and religious discussions of human goodness throughout history, fairness and equity have been highly valued. That we all deserve a fair chance—the core value of "justice"—is a timeless and near-universal belief.[2]

As we delved into the experiences of our interviewees, we observed a remarkable consistency in how our interviewees choose to view fairness in the world—the second choice along the path. The potency of two overarching beliefs about fairness stood out: first, the world is filled with ill fate and good fortune, and second, fairness equals access to opportunity.

## Ill Fate Versus Good Fortune

Intentionally, and usefully, our interviewees simplify the world. In the grand philosophical universe, they understand how some people are boxed in by life's luck of the draw. In their reality-checked wisdom, our interviewees know anyone, including themselves, could have been born into far more challenging circumstances. None of us gets to choose our parents, place of birth, or starting position in life. To our interviewees, one's anthropology is simple: pure chance. They do not recognize any selective birthright to entitlement. To them it's a cosmic crapshoot. We are born into advantage or disadvantage.[3]

Our grasp of this relativity matters as it influences our intrinsic attitude toward others. As we learned from our interviewees, if we see the disadvantaged as seemingly upstanding individuals beset by circumstance, we are led in the direction of compassion and a willingness to help. If, on the other hand, we see the disadvantaged as people whose circumstance is the result of their own personal flaws, poor choices and shortcomings, then we are likely to assign them blame and distance ourselves from them.

Ryan Hreljac understands this distinction. Over the course of a year, he raised $2,000 to build a well to provide clean water at the Angolo Primary School in northern Uganda in Africa. Of particular interest, Ryan was 6 years old.

As Ryan, 16 at the time of our interview, told us, "It all started in my first grade classroom when we were doing our annual charity project, canned food drives and all of that good stuff. That year we were raising money for developing countries. So my teacher brought in a list of things we could save for. Something like one cent would buy a pencil, $2 would buy a blanket, and so on. Then she got to the point where she said $70 would buy a well. She explained to us that they don't have clean water. I was 6 at the time, and it was the first time I actually really thought about anything. We were all confused by this. What do you mean they don't have water?"

Ryan's teacher explained to the class the simple arithmetic that added up to a colossal injustice. Too many people in the world had to walk 10 kilometers to get clean water, while more fortunate people, like the students in Ryan's classroom, only had to take about 10 steps to the nearest drinking fountain. "We didn't know what 10 kilometers was or the whole measurement thing, so our teacher said, 'It's something like 10,000 steps.'

"I remember that day and I just remember going from my classroom to the water fountain and counting the steps it took me to get there. I counted 10. I just thought it is really unfair that I am walking 10 steps and someone else is walking 10,000 steps just to get a drink of water."

Ryan understood the concept of fairness at age 6. Ten years later, as his work to provide clean water has broadened in scope, he understands it more deeply. "It's helping people, and I'm glad I'm still doing this today because of the benefits that have come out of it. It's great for everyone. When I was 9, my mom, dad, and I traveled to Uganda to see my well. When I wake up in the morning, a smile doesn't light up my face because I have clean water to drink, but they held a huge celebration. There was food, and there were people who came from 10 kilometers away. It was a huge celebration just because they had clean water."

What began as a seemingly implausible do-it-yourself improvement to the world resulted in a water well in a country 7,000 miles (11,000 kilometers) away, all because Ryan Hreljac felt a fierce passion for fairness: 10 steps versus 10,000 steps to get clean water. "I just thought it was really unfair," he said.

In many ways, the saga of humanity is an epic about the imbalances of fairness. The line between ill fate and good fortune is slender and fickle. Some people are blessed with good fortune right from the start and even along the way. Some are sucker punched by fate.

It can be hard to see the ill-fate side of the coin, especially if one is born with inherent advantage and open-range potential. In many middle- and upper-class communities in developed countries, children are spoon-fed the recipe for success beginning with preschool. In fact, the term itself is telling. Before school begins, there is school. Formal education is that important. For the privileged in the United States, college prep often begins in middle school. If you are not divined into such a success bound environment, your prospects are simply less from the outset. Context matters. In his book, *Outliers,* Malcolm Gladwell tells us success is the constant accumulation of advantage over several decades. He concludes that, "no one—not rock stars, not professional athletes, not software billionaires, and not even geniuses—ever makes it alone."[4]

But, if one starts out with nothing and is never given access to opportunities, as is the case for many people in developing countries, how can any advantage be accumulated? It's this contrast of opportunity that prompted Gordon Brown, the former British prime minister, to plead that Europe and America "come together to make sure the world is not just a more economically prosperous place, but a fairer place."[5]

## Access to Opportunity

Imagine that you have been diagnosed with a potentially fatal disease. Imagine also there is a treatment, but it's not available to you in the country where you live. Now contemplate these questions: What would you be willing to do to get to the country where you could be treated? Would you use all of your money? Would you plead to be treated? Would you put your life at further risk to get there? Now, in the midst of such anxiety and uncertainty, imagine the treatment—and maybe even a cure—being brought to you. That is exactly what Dr. David J. Winchester is committed to doing.

David J. Winchester is a nationally recognized surgical oncologist and expert in breast cancer surgery. He is a professor of surgery, holds an endowed chair, is a noted author, and serves with several national cancer organizations. Most important, David understands access to opportunity. On several occasions, he has left his busy practice and traveled to Russia and Latvia to perform lifesaving surgeries and teach leading-edge surgical techniques.

David told us that the first 2 years the team went to the Russian Ministry Railroad Hospital in Moscow, which serves as a centralized location for the care of railroad workers in the region. The hospital specializes in cancer treatment. He described striking disparities between operating room conditions in this hospital and hospitals in the United States.

"The Russian hospital is extremely impoverished," he said. "We were just saddened by the conditions in which the hospital staff work. They have operating rooms with windows that open to the outdoors. Most of their surgical equipment was from 50 years ago or older. They all had to provide their own scrubs, hats, and masks. We brought as much equipment and supplies as we could.

"I will never forget what happened after our first case," he continued. "We took off our latex surgical gloves, and as soon as they were off our hands and into the basket, they were picked up by the nurses to clean, recycle, and reuse. Everything we brought with us that we think of as disposable, they would try and reuse, from conductive pads to electric cautery pencils. It was just amazing how many needs they had."

With the care of cancer patients at a more formative stage in Russia, David said much of the focus of the trips has been on sharing the knowledge and technology of cancer surgery—in particular breast cancer surgery—an area in which there have been enormous strides in the United States in the past decade. Along with knowledge, the surgical team has brought hundreds of thousands of dollars of vital equipment and supplies, all desperately needed in Russia. "We typically don't check our bags, but we bring boxes of equipment instead," David said. "Last trip we brought 70 boxes of stuff. We used a lot of it during the operations and left whatever we didn't use."

By importing world-class medical care and knowledge to countries where health care is less advanced, David Winchester and his team are putting the idea of access to opportunity into action. "The first trip was set up with just one operating room," he told us. "It was my partner, myself, and a physician assistant. We did nine or 10 operations. The second trip we went to two operating rooms and we did 17. The third and fourth trips were about 13 operations each. We do a few days of operations as well as lectures." David added, "It seemed like we were helping the Russian doctors to help their patients and to be better doctors, and it was just a great thing to do. We also had a chance to learn from our Russian colleagues."

David Winchester is part of a small envoy bringing surgical expertise to places without access to skill and knowledge for fighting cancer. Similarly, Inderjit Khurana offers educational opportunities to children who otherwise would have had none, and Ryan Hreljac builds wells to provide clean water to people for whom access to clean water is severely limited. Sanphasit Koompraphant's story offers a different perspective. Sometimes fairness and access to opportunity require the passage of laws, which can be a long and often frustrating process.

Sanphasit was among the first to speak out against child abduction, trafficking, and prostitution in Thailand and the Mekong region, areas of the world in which such practices are not only rampant, but also well organized and commercially viable. He began his work in the early 1980s, working with the Center for the Protection of Children's Rights to rescue children in forced labor. Sanphasit described the horrific working conditions children endured before laws prevented such practices. "They start them at 12 years old. They have to work almost 14 hours a day. Many of the employers provide only two meals a day. They have to sleep on the floor." In the worst situations, Sanphasit said, children were beaten and even tortured. "So the situation at that moment was really bad, and there was no legal protection to this group of children," he added.

After initially focusing on helping children who had been exploited through child labor, in 1985 the Center became involved in combating the commercial sexual exploitation of children and in helping young people who had been abused or forced into prostitution. Child prostitution has historically been an enormous problem in Thailand, largely because it is so profitable. It is estimated that several million people earn their living directly or indirectly from the prostitution industry. In 1992, Sanphasit put the number of children in prostitution at 800,000, a figure for which he was roundly criticized by those seeking to protect the industry. Sadly, Sanphasit told us, it was not uncommon at the time for children as young as 12 or 13 to be forced into prostitution, mostly with migrant workers. At the most extreme, Sanphasit said, there was a "market" for children as young as 5 or 6.

Sanphasit discovered through his work with the Center that the children's families were at the root of many of the problems. He told us, "Many families who send their children to be a child laborer or child prostitute were not really poor, but they expect to get money from their children. So I start to work with the family. I found that there were a lot of cases of sexual abuse and physical abuse in the family." This discovery spurred a campaign against sexual abuse within families, but Sanphasit, who has a legal background, soon became convinced that a larger solution lay in changing the laws of the land. Without such laws, Sanphasit told us, there could be no safety for children and no opportunity for them to return to their families and receive the education that would offer them a chance for a better future.

"So in 1988 I started to explore our Thai legislation concerning children in every aspect, not just criminal law, family law, and child protection law," Sanphasit said. And he studied laws affecting not just Thai children, but also children from other countries, particularly Burma, who all too often crossed the border for forced labor and prostitution. At the time, Sanphasit explained, "The Thai government and the government of the country of origin [of the children] did not pay any attention to this group of victims. More than that, they did not try enough to prosecute or investigate trafficking kids."

Changing laws that governed long-ingrained and often socially accepted practices wasn't easy, however. In fact, the most significant child protection law wasn't passed until 2003. This groundbreaking law, the Child Protection Act, which Sanphasit played a key role in drafting, aimed to protect children under age 18 from all forms of abuse, exploitation, violence, and gross negligence. But acceptance and compliance hasn't come easily. As Sanphasit told the *Bangkok Post* in 2004, "We have to fight again and again because they [the government] said this law tries to limit or control children. But that is not the point. When children are in danger, someone must try to help and rescue them from that danger. That is a universal rule."

Our interviewees consistently define fairness in terms of access to opportunity. Opportunity changes the game for those who are afforded access, whether it's to education, clean water, surgery, or freedom from abuse. Access to opportunity offers a chance. Isolation from opportunity dictates stern limitations. Furthermore, if access to opportunity is afforded to some but not to others, additional difficulties can emerge. The late sociologist Robert Merton tells us social deviance occurs when a society encourages the same goals for all of its citizens without allowing everyone the same access to achieve them.[6] On such an uneven playing field, other problems can occur to offset the unfairness.

According to research by British epidemiologists Richard Wilkinson and Kate Pickett based on data from the World Bank, United Nations, World Health Organization, U.S. Census, and other sources, inequality in society undermines social trust and community life, leading to a host of problems. These problems include increased drug use, mental illness, teenage pregnancy, obesity, and violent crime. In an unequal society, Wilkinson and Pickett argue, the quality of life is diminished for everyone.[7]

Sure-footed about their sense of fairness, our interviewees articulate very clear perspectives. Sherri Kirkpatrick, who has worked for more than a quarter century to empower women and children in developing countries through health education and advocacy, told us, "Life is not fair. We have an extreme obligation to work toward a sense of fairness because we are so interconnected as a world."

Peter Samuelson, who created the Starlight Children's Foundation, said, "I don't think the world is fair. I believe that there are fundamentals of fairness that ought to be and are not. I believe that every human being has the right to an education. Every child has a right to health care. I believe everyone deserves a roof. I think that these are fundamentals of a civilization without which it's not really a very good civilization. How you treat your innocent, weakest members defines whether your whole damn civilization is worth anything. I don't think the world will ever be fair. All we can do is chip away at it."

Craig Kielburger, founder of Free The Children, puts fairness into this perspective: "Is it fair that 213 million children work in child labor? Absolutely not. Is it fair that 1.1 billion people live on less than $1.00 a day? Absolutely not. Equally, is it fair that we have so much? It is unfair, absolutely, without a doubt. What are we going to do about it? Fundamentally, that is the question. What is next? It requires us to reevaluate our priorities. How we give our time or our money. How we cast our ballot. From the philosophical question, is it fair or is it not fair, once we all agree that it's not fair, are we willing to take the next step, which requires that we fix it."

To Ryan Hreljac, the young man who spearheaded the building of hundreds of wells in more than a dozen countries, it is very simple. "Not everyone was born and has privileges where they can go to school and have three meals a day and have access to clean water. I guess for some people who do have those liberties, they have to think outside the box and help those who are less fortunate. Life isn't fair; the world isn't fair; but we can try and make it fair the best we can in our everyday lives."

Finally, Dr. Irving Williams, the pediatrician and public health specialist who has brought a multidisciplinary approach to health care in remote African communities, offers a broader perspective. "The blue sky that adorns the white sandy beaches in Miami is the same blue sky that adorns the white sandy beaches of Havana, Cuba. There is a need for us to get rid of these walls that separate us for no real reason at all," he said.

Whose responsibility is fairness? Our interviewees answer this question based on how they think about other people. They see some people as ill-fated by circumstances and lack of access to opportunities. They see how some people are advantaged while others are disadvantaged. This clear understanding is fundamental to their perspective on fairness.

In some well-imagined future, it all may be different. But for now, this is our world. Learning to live within our overwhelming array of challenges requires adopting one of two perspectives about fairness: There is nothing I can do about it. Or, I *can* matter. I *can* make a difference. It is this pivotal choice that we focus on in the next chapter.

## Clarifying Your Perspective on Fairness

1. Our interviewees have all accepted responsibility for righting some unfairness in the world. They see that some people, like the children outside the school gates in Bhubaneswar, are ill-fated through no fault of their own. But other people might have a different perspective. How do you think one's view of fairness might be influenced by one's own culture?

2. How do you think about people in need? Do you think that some people are advantaged while others are disadvantaged, or do you believe that everybody gets what he or she deserves? If you believe that a helping hand should be extended to those in need, do you believe helping the less advantaged is the role of government, or should it be left to faith-based groups, private charities, and individual citizens?

3. What about your own role in helping others? Are you inclined to step toward others or step back? Can you think of a time when you felt a strong sense of unfairness and decided to do something to help? Was there ever a time when you felt conflicting feelings when confronted with an instance of unfairness? For example, many people see homeless people on the streets on a daily basis, but few assume responsibility for the problem.

4. Do you agree that access to opportunity is at the core of fairness? Can you give other examples of disparities in society in terms of lack of opportunity between those who are advantaged and those who are disadvantaged?

5. What does it mean to be on the fringe of society? Have you ever felt that you were on the fringe? Have you ever been treated unfairly in terms of access to opportunity? How did this unfair treatment make you feel? Did it make you feel more inclined to do something to ensure that others don't have the same experience?

# Part Two

## Making A Commitment

*Unless someone like you*

*cares a whole awful lot,*

*nothing is going to get better.*

*It's not.*

—Theodor Geisel, "Dr. Seuss,"
*The Lorax*

# 3

# Believe We Can Matter

*It's a Gift That I Have, and I Use It*

Mama Liz pulled several worms out of the young girl. They were all about the same size, maybe 8 inches (20 centimeters) long, about the size of a small garter snake. The girl was perhaps 4 or 5 years old, no one knew for sure, not even the girl herself. She had simply showed up one morning at the Children's Center in Idweli, Tanzania. And because the village had several hundred children who had lost both parents, usually to AIDS, and because the center had already exceeded the limit the village governing board had set for its capacity to accept and care for children, specifically the "neediest" children of the village, Mama Liz fed her as best she could and reluctantly told her she would have to go home. So the young girl went home. But she came back the next morning, and the morning after that, and the morning after that. So finally Mama Liz let her stay. This wasn't the first time Mama Liz had ignored official policy, and it certainly wouldn't be the last. So she helped the young girl wash, treated the sores on her head, wrote her name at the top of a fresh page in the loose-leaf notebook that served as a medical chart, and dewormed her.

Mama Liz walked down toward the kitchen area where the food was prepared for the 54 children who lived in the Children's Center, and a small band of children walked with her. Wherever Mama Liz went, a small band of children went with her. Typically, one child would be bouncing the ball that had become the main plaything for the center's children. Several children would be watching the bouncer try a new under-the-leg maneuver while they waited for their turn. Several would be very close or clinging to Mama Liz's clothing, and if she were sitting there would be one in her lap. Several other children would simply be there, joining in the chatter, simply present because if anything interesting were going to happen, Mama Liz was likely to be somehow involved. The group moved in a small cloud of dust circling their ankles. Almost everything that happened outdoors in this sub-Saharan village stirred up dust. They were headed toward the cooking area. The cooking was done mostly with an open fire and grill, and was roofed against the infrequent rains. But when the air didn't move, the smoke gathered and stayed beneath the roof, and the villagers who did the cooking were finding it very hard to cook and breathe at the same time. The problem was eventually solved when Mama Liz raised the money to install a ventilation system in the cooking area.

Mama Liz is a problem solver. She spent a lot of her time trying to make things better, usually for the kids. She ran the dispensary at the center. She treated malaria, tuberculosis, malnutrition, infection, and an endless variety of other problems associated with the neediest children of the village. For the really tough problems, she could consult the village's doctor, and though he was a very competent and caring doctor, he also took care of all the children and adults in Idweli and five other villages in his ward. So Mama Liz was the orphanage's nurse who helped out by treating villagers, as well. She also taught classes for the center's children and the other village children in the center's preschool. And she helped some of the older children get the required uniforms so they could attend the village's regular school. She started women's groups that dealt with problems such as teachers who "caned" children and used children to perform labor on the teachers' farms. She also taught the young girls of the village that they didn't have to have sex simply because a boy demanded it, one of the many cultural norms uncritically accepted by the children. Mama Liz was always poking away at uncritically accepted norms, especially if the norms dealt with issues of cleanliness or any behavior that she knew was directly related to contracting or spreading disease.

Mama Liz is the affectionate name given to Liz Clibourne by the children in the village of Idweli, Tanzania. Liz's home is actually in Hawaii. She describes herself as a "burned out nurse." She works in a hospital—that is, she works there until she has accumulated enough money, usually $15,000 to $20,000, and then, with the help of her grown-up children and friends, she goes to Africa. The money allows her to help the children as well. "I could live over there on a couple hundred bucks a month, personal expenses," Liz explained. "But that doesn't give me any money to buy the things you need to buy. I bought shoes. I bought the doctors medicine. You had 60 kids there, and there were kids in the village that needed stuff."

Liz finds places where she can volunteer her time and effort. She has been on a medical mission in Honduras, and she spent 7 months in Ghana working at an orphanage with 105 children. She was the first person we interviewed for this research project. At that time, she was back in the United States, having returned from her second trip to Africa. She returned to the hospital, worked, saved enough money for a return trip to Africa, and at this writing is back in Tanzania. According to one of the e-mails she sends to her friends and supporters, she has been helping a group of nuns paint the buildings that will be used as an orphanage.

Mama Liz's impact on the village in Idweli has been considerable. In fact, members of the two U.S.-based foundations that had helped the villagers build the center, as well as members of a research team who were there to study the impact of the center on the psychological, social, and physical well-being of the children, had all started talking about "the Liz effect." This refers to very apparent and dramatic changes in the well-being of the center children, ranging from health and physical well-being to their optimism about the future and their belief in their own ability to impact that future.[1]

Liz Clibourne's willingness to go to far-off places where her skills are desperately needed, and her success in solving the problems she finds there, are rooted in a deep belief that she can have an impact. This third choice along the path, which we call *believe we can matter,* is consistent among all our interviewees.[2] It is here where we see how our interviewees move along the inner path of social responsibility, from the emotions of empathy and feelings of fairness, beyond the pull of rationalization, to choosing to do something. It's where they talk to themselves less about hopelessness and helplessness and more about the possibilities, and it is within the possibilities where they see their own ability to make a difference. Here they find the next step in the logic that leads them to transform a good intention into a good deed. It is in believing they can matter that they assume responsibility for those in need and mentally step into those places left empty by the doubts and hesitations of others. We learned from our interviewees that believing they can matter is influenced by a three-part interlocking perspective: how they view a problem, how they see themselves, and how they think about the future.

## Focus on the Person, Not the Problem

Big problems, those pervasive challenges at a global or community level, can appear impossible to do anything about, let alone solve. In their broadest contexts, they probably are. After all, how is it possible to reconcile hundreds of millions of people going hungry every day? Or child sex trade, drug trafficking, or the inadequate availability of education and health care? Or wars fueled by religious disagreements and ethnic hatreds so personalized that no outsider can even understand the problem, let alone help? These are pernicious problems that are so large they cannot be coerced into going away and so complex as to discourage any attempt to try. For many people, a numbing to the problem occurs, referred to as psychophysical numbing, when the magnitude of the problem seems so overwhelming. This condition can lead to the devaluing of human life and a failure to do anything to help.[3]

Perhaps it is for this reason that our interviewees focus on the person, not the problem. In the faces of individuals, they find focus and solvability.[4] Individuals, each with their own backstory, offer a microcosm of a macro problem. All of a sudden a problem that is huge, disorienting, and intractable is somehow reduced in size and made possible to address. At an individual level it's even possible to witness progress.

Nicholas D. Kristof, a *New York Times* columnist, makes a similar point that people are more likely to help others when they see the person, not the larger problem.[5] Kristof cites a study by Paul Slovic, a psychology professor at the University of Oregon, in which people give generously to help Rokia, a 7-year-old girl in Mali, Africa, suffering from malnutrition, but when Rokia's plight is placed in the larger context of hunger in Africa, they are much less likely to contribute.

Slovic finds, as we did, that people are more likely to help others when a connection is made with an individual person as, for example, Craig Kielburger did with the murdered Pakistani boy. Slovic writes about the need for people to "feel" the reality of human suffering before they are willing to help, which, he says, happens most powerfully when that suffering is represented by a person with a face and a name. This conviction that their efforts will indeed make a difference because the problem is downsized to a manageable level is one of the key determinants in our interviewees believing they can matter. They are shrewd interpreters of what is doable and achievable.

Mama Liz described to us just such a doable focus. "I really get attached to the kids. A lot of people here in America worry about kids in general. Over in Africa or in third-world countries, I worry about kids in particular, because I live with them, and I was taking care of them. So I am worried about these particular kids. I'd like to get some of them, as many as I can, educated and on their way."

Liz illustrated this focus by describing what is called the leaving exam in Tanzania. All children have one opportunity to pass the exam, which is given at the end of standard seven, the last year of primary school. If they pass the leaving exam, they have the opportunity to go on to the government school for further education. If they don't pass, their formal education ends. Liz told us that in her first year at the Children's Center, only two students passed the exam. By the second year, she said, "They did so much better. We had more passing grades than nonpassing grades." Liz's presence in the community had made a measurable and meaningful difference in the educational success of the students.

Liz is not trying to fix Africa. She can't. But while she was there she could help and care about the 54 kids at the Children's Center.

This specific group of children is what provided a focus for her energy and effort. It helped distinguish what was important and what was not. It helped order the priorities. It helped her advocate a position, confront authority, persist in the face of resistance, and question even tradition and culture when those ways of thinking accepted or condoned practices that exploited or abused these children. The children were each her responsibility. Not all children, just these 54 children.

The narrowing of focus, from a problem to a person, is critical to energizing a pragmatic optimism. When we focus on the person it allows possibilities because we don't have to grapple with the whole problem. It's equivalent to turning "I can't solve world hunger" into "I can feed someone today."

None of our interviewees is overwhelmed by the size of the problems they have chosen to address because they adopt a practical focus. As we have seen so far, while Victor Dukay cannot solve the problem of children who have lost both parents to AIDS, he was able to focus on 60 orphans in Africa. Inderjit Khurana focused on the children at the train stations, not on the 20,000 children in Bhubaneswar who are not in school. Reflecting her experiences in Haiti, and directly to the point, the title of Susie Krabacher's book is *Angels of a Lower Flight: One Woman's Mission to Save a Country . . . One Child at a Time*. Among our interviewees, the first of the three perspectives that influence believing we can matter is a highly consistent and useful way of viewing a large social challenge: focus on the person, not the problem.

## Know What You Have to Offer

How we choose to see ourselves is a critical factor in whether we decide to devote our time and effort to helping others. As we have learned, those who believe they can matter have a powerful understanding of their own strengths and interests, and they acknowledge that those strengths can make a real and significant difference in the lives of people in need. Sometimes, however, as the stories that follow demonstrate, how we can best help is not immediately apparent. Rather, it comes to us with time, experience, and reflection.

Gerry Sieck was a successful executive at Baxter Healthcare, a large multinational company based in Illinois. As assistant general counsel and corporate secretary, his life was filled with interesting challenges and opportunities for growth, which raises a fundamental question. Why, at the age of 42 and at the height of his career, would Gerry give up a high-paying position with a prestigious company to teach middle school students in inner-city Chicago? The answer begins with a fourth grade girls' basketball team.

Gerry told us he came home from work one night and read a letter from his daughter's school that said there would be no fourth grade girls' basketball team that year because they didn't have a coach. Gerry easily could have said, "That's too bad," and sat down to have dinner with his family after a long day. Instead, he said to himself, "That's not going to happen. If no one is going to coach the kids, I'll coach. They have to have a basketball team." So Gerry called the school the next day and volunteered to help. He also called a friend whose daughter was on the team; together Gerry and his friend ended up coaching the girls' basketball team not only in fourth grade, but every year until the girls graduated from eighth grade.

It's not surprising that Gerry volunteered his services; he had spent a lifetime assuming responsibility and helping others. One of 11 children, Gerry was raised on a 5-acre (2-hectare) vegetable farm in the middle of Roselle, Illinois. "I saw my parents relatively poor," Gerry told us. "They never went out to dinner. They never had any new clothes. I never had anything new my whole life. We had a very humble upbringing."

What's more, what little Gerry's parents did have, they gave away. Gerry remembers that his mother, who went to church regularly, would always pass the same homeless woman walking along the way. "My mom would stop the car every day and pick her up," Gerry recalled. "She would get in our car, my mom would tell us to move over, and she would drive her to church."[6] Gerry also told us that from the time he was a senior in high school, his family always had someone living with them who couldn't take care of themselves. "Sometimes it was a relative, sometimes it wasn't, but they always had someone in the house. I was taught to be charitable to people who need it more than I do. People in need—take care of them. My parents weren't teachers, but they certainly could have been."

Gerry learned the lesson of helping those in need from his parents, and he also learned the value of hard work. Gerry's father had a vision for his children. They were not going to get into trouble in the big city. "We were going to farm vegetables to pay for our school tuitions," Gerry explained. "So that was our job. From the time I was in fifth grade, I paid for all of my school education, all the way through law school. When I was 7 years old, I got my first job mowing lawns. I had five lawn mowing jobs, and I still took care of my vegetable crop."

Fortunately for Gerry, he was accustomed to not taking the easy way out because coaching the fourth grade girls' basketball team was not an easy assignment. His daughter attended a small Catholic school that did not have its own gym. So the team had to borrow gym time from other schools and facilities. Their practices were held on Friday nights from 7 to 9, and Sunday mornings from 7 to 9. "Just the worst times for practice," Gerry said. "Just the times I didn't want to be with fourth graders practicing basketball." But Gerry soon realized he was having as much fun as the girls, and he stayed with it, even coaching his younger daughter's team for another 2 years.

Gerry and the other father who coached with him—a Big Ten running back in college—had very different philosophies of how to instruct the girls, most of whom probably never would be star athletes. Their approaches were based on vastly different experiences growing up. "My friend never experienced anything but success in sports," Gerry explained. "I almost never experienced success." Gerry realized that for most of the girls what would be most important would be for them to experience teamwork, commitment, and sportsmanship. "I really worked on teaching the kids about working together as a team, learning, listening, cooperating," Gerry said, "all the things that you try to teach them. The other coach was more focused on teaching them how to play."

Gerry told us he derived great satisfaction from giving those girls who were not star players a chance at opportunities they might never have experienced. "I remember games when I would put the five worst girls in if we were winning by a lot. Then I would put one or two starter girls in just to bring in the ball, and I told them, all I want you to do is pass to the other three, and they would do all of the shooting. To see those girls, who could never shoot a basket during the game, just light up and have their teammates cheer for them. It was gratifying for me."

Coaching girls' basketball was not only satisfying for Gerry, it was also instructive. He realized in a deep and meaningful way that he was good with kids—unusually good. "I could see that I could connect with the kids. I was pretty successful in getting those kids with their mediocre skills or almost no skills to improve. They did listen to me. They wanted to learn, and they wanted to try what I was teaching them. So I felt as though I could get results with the kids. I was connected with them." This insight prompted Gerry to think more seriously about something he had been considering for some time—that his next step in life should be as a teacher.

Gerry realized his experiences in sports as a child paralleled his experiences as a student. Despite his later success, Gerry often lacked motivation in school, and it was his teachers who were the coaches that encouraged him to do better. "So I wondered, how many other kids are there out there like me who might think, you know what, I'm just a bad student. I can't go to college or law school. I can't do that kind of thing. It was teachers in the past that told me that I was better than I realized if I would work at it. I thought if I had the opportunity to work with a few hundred kids, and maybe 20 of them are like me, or even 10 of them are like me, then it's worth it for me."

So Gerry left Baxter Healthcare and returned to DePaul University for 2 years to become a middle school teacher. "Middle school kids are the most vulnerable," Gerry explained. "They're tough one day, they are vulnerable the next day, they want a hug, and sometimes they are defiant. It's a very, very tender age. And that to me is the most rewarding part of teaching, when I can engage them and they realize they are smarter than they think they are." He added, "That's how I got from basketball to teaching. I realized I can do this all day with many more kids."

Gerry did his student teaching at Thurgood Marshall Middle School, an inner-city Chicago school with a diverse mix of students—Hispanic, African American, Asian, Native American. He taught social studies to some 100 seventh graders, and it was exactly what he was aspiring to do.

Then after learning that his student-teaching mentor would be taking an extended maternity leave the following school year, Gerry offered to assume her teaching responsibilities while she was away—an offer that was embraced by the teacher and principal. The opportunity appealed to Gerry because he would have the same seventh graders, with whom he had connected, as eighth graders the following year. More important, Gerry said, had he not stepped in, his students would have had a parade of substitute teachers. "I couldn't let that happen. It not only would have been very frustrating for the students and teachers, but it would have been a lost year of education."

Gerry knows he cannot fix a school system, but he can make a tangible impact on 120 or so students by turning them on to learning, keeping their interest by maintaining an orderly classroom, and helping them experience the rewards of accomplishment. Equally gratifying, if he can help 20 or even 10 students who might be like he was by getting them to work a little harder and believe in themselves, then he knows he has mattered in someone's life.

"Teaching is not only the hardest job I ever had, but the best job I ever had," Gerry said. "The last few years have been the happiest and most rewarding in my professional career. The reward I get from interacting with teens, seeing a light bulb go on in their heads when I get them to realize that they just got something, that's really cool."

Gerry was a very successful corporate attorney before moving into the classroom. He's still very successful, and it all began with Gerry recognizing what he had to offer. As he put it, "I am a really good teacher, and I really connect with kids. It's natural for me. It's a gift that I have and I use it."

Gerry's success as a teacher stemmed from an exceptionally strong match between leadership style and context, the basis of what is known as Fiedler's *contingency theory* of leadership. As the pioneering management psychologist wrote, "A leader who is liked, accepted, and trusted by his members [in this case, the students] will find it easy to make his influence felt."[7] For Gerry, his gift for connecting with young people and helping them fulfill their potential, which he first identified as the coach of a girls' basketball team, came to full realization in the context of an inner-city middle school classroom.

Interestingly, sometimes we are not even aware of the gift we have to offer. We are not aware of our ability to make a difference. Such was the insight arrived at by Bill Sergeant, who made a far-reaching and lasting contribution to the global effort to eradicate polio.

It's worth noting from the outset that Bill was neither a doctor nor did he have a medical background. Furthermore, Bill began his health care effort at the age of 75, some 15 years after he retired as director of security for a weapons production and research installation in Oakridge, Tennessee. Yet, Bill received an honorary doctorate from a university in India; he was made part of the Fries Foundation at Stanford University for his work in global public health; the Centers for Disease Control and Prevention honored him; and the Rotarians in Knoxville, Tennessee, erected a statue of Bill holding a child in a downtown city park—all in his retirement years.

It wasn't all that long ago that polio was a devastatingly crippling and even fatal disease. The first polio vaccine was developed by Dr. Jonas Salk and declared "safe, effective, and potent" on April 12, 1955. The oral vaccine was developed by Dr. Albert Sabin and licensed in 1962. Today, only access to the vaccine prevents polio from being eliminated throughout the world. It is the access to this lifesaving immunization to which Bill Sergeant devoted more than a decade of his life.

Bill told us his public service began when he was called to active duty in the Army during World War II, straight out of military school. He served as a provost marshal, or military chief of police, which prepared him for his director of security position as a civilian when the war ended. In 1947, Bill joined the Rotary Club in Oakridge.

Dedicated to the Rotarian credo of "Service Above Self," Bill willingly and repeatedly assumed increasing responsibilities and performed each one well. Then, in 1994, something unusual occurred. Rotary International asked Bill if he would head the new International PolioPlus Committee. Bill was a trustee of the Rotary Foundation at the time, and he was charged with overseeing a portfolio of international projects, one of which was the polio program. But Bill said no.

"For the first time in my Rotary life, I said no, I wouldn't do it," Bill told us. "I would be on the committee, but I would not head it. And then, the strangest thing happened. A week later, they appointed me chairman anyway. I've never heard of that. I've heard of people twisting your arm. Would you like to think it over? But there was no one to talk to. I just got a letter saying this committee agreed that you are the chairman. So, I thought, oh well, I will just do it for a year." One year, of course, eventually turned into 12.

As Bill explained in our interview, "My reluctance to head the committee was simply because I thought there were a lot of technical aspects about the eradication of polio for which I was not qualified, and that I must know something about the technical aspects to do the job. I took the job, and 3 months after I was in, I knew the problem wasn't technical at all. It didn't have anything to do with it. The trouble was with planning right and managing right, and that was my forte.

"I had experience in managing things without knowing all the technical aspects," Bill continued. "My work as director of security was interrupted in 1950 when a National Guard battalion was called up from the federal service and I took it to Korea. It was an engineer combat battalion. I was a lieutenant colonel. As the commanding officer of the battalion, I took them into combat. I was the only officer that was not an engineer. I took this battalion into combat and was decorated for it. I used the same kinds of principles that I used with anything else. I was able to put my finger on the right person to do the right job. I found it worked out in a military situation, as well as in a civilian position."

In the first year that Bill led the International PolioPlus Committee's effort to free the world of polio, he began identifying ways to more effectively achieve this ambitious but essential goal. The biggest challenge, Bill discovered, was to convince people in the organization that the battle against polio wasn't over. What was needed, Bill decided, was to involve Rotarians more directly in the eradication effort, and so a new program called PolioPlus Partners was formed.

"The effect of PolioPlus Partners was significant in the amount of money it produced, but that wasn't nearly as important as what else happened," Bill said.

Realizing that the challenge of getting the vaccine in the child's mouth would be more compelling to Rotarians than just raising money to pay for vaccines, Bill tapped into all the resources available from the global Rotarian community to help make this happen. From Rotarians in Africa and Asia—where the polio virus persists—he got help with the daily tasks associated with immunization drives, especially assistance with the transportation of indigent and isolated mothers and children to and from immunization centers. From wealthier Rotarians in the United States, Canada, and Europe—regions in which polio has been eradicated—he was able to assemble and galvanize a large fundraising base. Many of these Rotarians became so interested in the effort that they eventually volunteered to travel abroad to assist with the administration and dispensation of the vaccine. "They wanted the thrill, because it is, of putting that vaccine in the child's mouth," Bill said. And once the Rotarians returned home, Bill added, they became a powerful voice for mobilizing still more support.

The ease of administering the oral polio vaccine made it possible for Rotarians to be directly involved in immunizing children. Bill told us about his own hands-on experience: "When you have to do something with a needle, it's a problem. The child doesn't want to go back, and adults don't want to go back either to get a needle stuck in their children. But I've seen long lines to get the polio vaccine. The little kids, they don't know what's going on up at the other end of the line. The only thing they know is the people up in front, whatever they are doing to them, they aren't crying. If they heard them screaming and hollering up at the front end, they would try and figure out some way to get out of the line. It's easier if it is something to put in their mouths. The vaccine has a sweetener; it tastes good. I had a little kid in my arms, and I gave him the vaccine. He opened his mouth to see if he could have more. It doesn't hurt at all. We also paint their fingernail. We give them a piece of candy and say, 'I'll give you another piece of candy if you can find the kid that's not painted.' They run off looking for one that is not painted." Not surprisingly, Rotarians also provided the candy used to reward kids who have been vaccinated.

Bill Sergeant sometimes traveled more than 100 times a year to Europe, Asia, Africa, and throughout the United States to help vaccinate children. In 2001, 575 million children—almost one-tenth of the world's population—received the polio vaccine. Reported polio cases for that year were down by more than 99 percent since 1988. The National Immunization Days can now accommodate as many as 150 million children under the age of 5 in a single day. More than 500,000 cases of polio are now prevented each year by the Global Polio Eradication Initiative, an effort spearheaded by Rotary's leadership. Or bringing it down to a more individual level, when Bill began his job, some 1,000 children were paralyzed by polio every single day somewhere in the world. In 2006, about 1,000 children a year were paralyzed by the disease—still too many, but a vast improvement.

As chairman of the International PolioPlus Committee and one of only three people in the world appointed by the director general of the World Health Organization (WHO) to figure out how to make the immunization process more effective, Bill Sergeant made a tremendous contribution to humanity. He did so by understanding and applying what he had to offer. A representative of WHO said of Bill in remarks recognizing his work, "Bill has lived up to his name of Sergeant in the battle against polio. Bill Sergeant remains a towering force and a legend in global polio eradication. His vision and leadership have been unmatched."

Believing we can matter begins with knowing, as well as acknowledging, we have something to offer. Our interviewees know themselves. They know what they are good at and what they like doing. In each case, once they recognized what they had to offer and found the right context for their efforts, our interviewees also realized they had the power to somehow change the future for someone else.

## You Can Change the Future

Kathy Magee uses her skills as a nurse and clinical social worker to dramatically improve the futures of children around the world, one child at a time. Along with her husband, Dr. William Magee, a plastic and craniofacial surgeon, Kathy brings a team of surgical experts to countries where the prospects are limited for correcting cleft palate and cleft lip, a serious but highly treatable congenital malformation. A baby born with cleft palate and cleft lip has an opening in the lip, the roof of the mouth, or the soft tissue in the back of the mouth. Without surgery, a child would have this condition for life, leading to a host of medical and social problems. The fact is, however, in extreme cases, without surgery there is a good chance the child would not survive, as a cleft palate prevents an infant from properly swallowing food.

Bill Magee was in private practice in Virginia helping children with cleft palates and other deformities, and Kathy was a pediatric nurse when they first got the opportunity to travel to the Philippines along with a group of medical volunteers to repair children's cleft lips and cleft palates. There they discovered hundreds of children suffering from these deformities.

"We hit four sites. We would provide surgery for 40 to 60 children in a day or two and then we would hop to another site," Kathy told us. "The last area we went to was Naga City in the Province of Camarines Sur. It was a very rural site for us. The Mayon volcano was there, and there were rice paddies with people working in them. It was just a very, very poor area. Who knows how old the people were. They were just beaten by the sun and the work.

"When we arrived at the hospital we were not prepared for what we encountered," Kathy continued. "There must have been 200 to 300 kids waiting for us with their families. Now mind you, there are only 18 of us. We all just huddled in the middle of the room. It was hot, we were dripping, and we just looked at each other like there is no way we are going to be able to help them all. We can help 40 kids, but there are 300, all with facial deformities. We said, 'Okay, let's just do whatever we can.' We took my 14-year-old daughter with us and taught her how to assist in the OR. She worked 14 hours a day. She fainted once. We knew we turned away 250 children. The hospital administrator said, 'If you can think about coming back some day, these children will still be here. They will be 5 years older, but they will still be here.'"

Kathy and Bill knew they had to mobilize support so that they could return and help these children—and so many more. "So, we talked about it on the flight going home," Kathy recalled. "What can we do? Who can we get? This is what really kicked off Operation Smile, because the team that we were with did not go back. We gathered friends; we met with plastic surgeons in Europe. We met plastic surgeons in all of the areas we studied so we could dial up specialists. My husband worked with Johnson & Johnson, and he asked if they could give us sutures. They said, no problem, we can do that for you. Everybody started to come around saying yes."

Operation Smile, which is now a worldwide charity dedicated to improving the lives of children and young adults, started in the Philippines in 1982. Over time, the organization was invited to help in more and more areas. "A letter from Mother Teresa asked if we could go to India," Kathy said. "Then we were asked to go to Colombia, and so forth." Operation Smile now has a presence in 60 countries. "We have operated on over 160,000 children, and we have educated hundreds and hundreds of people along the way," Kathy noted with justifiable pride.

Most memorable for Kathy was her second trip to Vietnam. "When we arrived at the hospital, a mother grabbed my hand and took me to a room. You could tell this mother was frantic. She took my hand, and we went to a room and I thought, oh my gosh, are you kidding me? The child was 7 or 8 days old and was pretty limp. She knew and I knew this child was going to die. She was just pulling my arm. She picked up the baby, and she was spoon-feeding it with a little water and rice milk. I thought, how on earth was the baby existing? The baby had a cleft palate.

"The woman was an older mom, and this was her only child," Kathy continued. "She was desperate. I went to the team and said 'What are we going to do?' They said, 'We can't do anything because this child will die. Do we want this child to die under surgery? No, we cannot come here and do that.' There were a couple of dentists with us, and they were doing obturators. Those are little appliances, like an orthodontic appliance, that you put in the roof of the mouth. They cost about 35 cents. If we can't fix the palate right away, the obturator locks the roof of the mouth so the child can eat, because they are all malnourished. The dentist finally said, 'We are going to do this. It's not going to be easy because it's a 7-day-old infant and is the obturator going to stay in? We will do our best.' The mom was just so happy that we were working on something to keep her child alive. It was the last thing we did before we left Vietnam. The next year when we went back, I got off the plane and went to the hospital. The mom was the first person standing in line with a fat little 1-year-old, who now we could do surgery on." Kathy paused and then added, "How many times does someone actually get to change a life? That's what it's all about."

Our interviewees do not expect or promise to cross the finish line for those they help. They merely give them a chance at a better future—in the form of tools, skills, and opportunities—so they might cross it themselves, one by one. It's Mama Liz helping 54 African students get an increased chance to pass a one-time test that determines continuing or stopping education in Tanzania. It's Gerry Sieck helping 10 or 20 inner-city students to realize their potential. It's Bill Sergeant ensuring that millions of children are protected by the polio vaccine from crippling illness or death. It's Kathy Magee providing the dramatic difference cleft palate surgery makes in the life of an infant, child, or adult. The futures of many individuals were different because of Liz, Gerry, Bill, and Kathy. Our interviewees are able to envision two futures, one with and one without their help.[8] It's clear to them that the future with their help is a vastly improved one for many people in need. Consistently and repeatedly, our interviewees changed the future for someone else.

Our interviewees believe they can matter. This belief leads them to being open to an opportunity to make a difference, the fourth choice along the inner path of social responsibility and the focus of our next chapter.

## Can You Make a Difference?

1. Our own research and that of others has shown that people are more willing to help others when they are able to see the person, not the larger problem. For example, Liz Clibourne talks about helping 54 children in Africa, which she can do, rather than every African child in need, which would clearly be an overwhelming, if not impossible, challenge. Can you think of a time when you decided you could make a difference because you had scaled a large problem down to size?

2. Attorney Gerry Sieck became involved in teaching after coaching girls' basketball proved to him that he was a gifted teacher. If you've been involved in a volunteer opportunity, what strengths did you bring? Did you know beforehand that you had those strengths, or, like Gerry, did a particular experience give you clarity about your talents or skills that would be of value to others?

3. People like Kathy Magee, who brings her nursing and organizational skills to young people with facial deformities in the Philippines and other countries, have a clear sense that what they do will make life better for the people they help. Can you think about a social problem that you would like to help solve? How would your involvement change the future for other people? Why is envisioning a better future for people, or even one person, in need so important?

# 4

# Open to an Opportunity

*Busy in Baghdad*

T wo Black Hawk helicopters lifted out of Baghdad, buzzing their way at treetop level up to Mosul and down to Tikrit, picking up various soldiers and press before making it to Samarra. Located midway between Mosul and Baghdad on Highway 1, Samarra is right in the middle of the Sunni Triangle, about 40 miles (64 kilometers) north of Fallujah. Some 30 days earlier, the first Infantry Division of the American military did a house-to-house sweep through Samarra, eliminating as many insurgents as they could. It was a critical first step in taking back the city from insurgents, but only a first step in this phase of the Iraq war.

During this 2-hour ride, Major Larry Bradley knew none of this on his first day in Iraq. Equally important, he did not know his path would cross with a young Iraqi boy named Ali. All he knew was what had transpired during the past few months. He had arrived back home in New York on July 21 from a business meeting in Chicago, and his wife had handed him a telegram. After he opened it, she asked Larry repeatedly, "What does it mean?" Finally, the graduate of West Point simplified it for his wife, just as it was simplified in his own mind: "Orders are orders."

Larry knew he was well trained at West Point and that he had gained invaluable experience during his 5 years of active duty. But he also knew he was 39 years old and had not worn a uniform in more than 12 years. As a major in the Army Reserve, he wore a business suit when recruiting for the academy. He knew he had three small children who were 8, 6, and 1. He knew that just a few months before he was a manager of supply chain solutions at Cardinal Health, where his mission was serving hospitals in the New York region. But that was July 21. On August 31 he left for training at Fort Benning, Georgia, and now it was November 27, 2004, the day after Thanksgiving. His mission, he was told, was to lead and train Iraqi soldiers. He and his unit of 10 Americans would be embedded with a battalion of 750 Iraqis in Samarra.

The Black Hawks finally made their way to Samarra. Larry remembered that day clearly. "We hovered over this American base, and I'm staring at it out of the helicopter. I look at the door gunner, because it doesn't look that bad. There were Bradley fighting vehicles. There were M1 tanks. You can see soldiers around. I said, 'All right, this isn't going to be so bad.' The door gunner looks at me and shakes his head and signals, 'This isn't you.' We hovered there for a while, and then we proceeded to fly another 5 minutes north, where we hovered over a triple standard barbed wire fenced base. It had about six towers in the middle of nowhere. There was trash blowing everywhere. There were no buildings, only a few tents. There was what looked like a bombed out building that had a couple of American Humvees in front of it. The helicopters hovered. They wouldn't land because the sand was too soft. The door gunner said, 'Get out of the helicopter. This is it.' We threw our stuff out of the helicopter. We were standing there and two Humvees pulled up. They said, 'Are you Major Bradley?' and I said, 'Yes.' They said, 'Throw your stuff in the Humvee. We're going on patrol in downtown Samarra. You are leading the other vehicle, and here is the map. You've got one company of Iraqis that are following you. We're doing a raid, and do you got any questions?'"

Larry and his company stayed out for 10 hours, all night long. The following days were equally grueling. "My entire team earned their combat infantry badge on day 3 of being on the ground," he said.

"Car bombs, shootings go on all around us. We were in a kind of industrial sector, so we went through a lot of buildings that we were clearing as potential car-bomb-making factories."

Back in the States, Larry's coworkers had formed their own fighting force, calling themselves Larry's Army. Their mission was to support Larry and his unit any way they could. They raised money for a satellite phone and airtime, so the men could speak with their families. Cell phones were banned where Larry and his men were based because they were used by insurgents to detonate car bombs. They sent soccer balls and pencil cases. The team sent Q-tips and cotton balls to help clean sand from the men's weapons. They sent pastrami and cheese from a deli in the Bronx, and every issue of the *New York Post* so the men could keep up with events back home, especially the Yankees. They took Larry's son to Yankees and Knicks games. They helped fix his wife's computer so she could receive e-mail and share photos of their kids. Soon, the team grew to nearly 100 people and included Larry's friends, colleagues, and customers.

Back in Iraq, Larry and his men patrolled with Iraqi soldiers every day, sometimes twice a day, in the city of Samarra, fighting a counterinsurgency battle for more than 3 months. Each mission was dangerous, and they were shot at regularly. Nothing was simple. Nothing was easy. Sometimes they were hit by insurgent fire in their Humvees as soon as they left the barbed wire gate of their base. While out on patrol, Larry and his men found their food vendor's truck on the side of the road. The food vendor and his 15-year-old son were both shot and killed. The water vendor was killed. Ten Iraqi civilians were hanged on the bridge leading down to Baghdad because of their support of the American base.

As Larry told us, "The first month the Iraqis trained 26 policemen. Two days after they graduated, 10 of them were assassinated in the police station. The other 16 quit, and we went back to square one. So my Iraqi soldiers went in and occupied the police station until we could train more."

But from the beginning Larry led by example. He never asked his men to do anything he wouldn't do himself, including riding the gun, a 50-caliber machine gun mounted on top of the Humvee. As the son of a New York City fireman who was "always being told what is right and what is wrong," Larry also emphasized doing the right thing.

"When I introduced myself to my team and whenever I talked with my guys, I just said, 'While we are here we are going to do the right thing. People know what the right thing is. You know in your gut when you are doing something if it's right. There is just something inside of you. It's something inside everybody. While we are here we are going to complete our mission, but along the way we are going to do the right thing. At the end of this we can all look at ourselves in the mirror—tomorrow, 10 to 20 years from now—and say we did what was right and have no regrets. Otherwise, things will haunt you for the rest of your life.' I was the leader of this team, and I was responsible for these nine U.S. soldiers."

At the end of February, Larry, along with one of his sergeants, was transferred to Taji Base, near Baghdad, to take over as the advisor team leader to the 5th Iraqi Army Battalion. It was just outside of Baghdad on March 20 that Larry came across an Iraqi boy named Ali, and all of his values were squarely tested.

"We were doing a raid in a village just north of Baghdad, and we found all kinds of improvised explosive device materials," Larry recalled. "We were going to speak to the sheik of the village to set up a town hall meeting. On the way, a father and a little boy walked up to us, and he pointed to the kid. His lips were purple, and his fingers were all blown up like lollipops. The kid had obvious respiratory problems. He was huffing and puffing just from walking up to us. I called my medic forward and had him evaluate the kid. He just stuck in our heads. We went back that night, talked about him, and said, what can we do? We threw some ideas around."

A few days later, on Easter Sunday, Larry and his men hatched a plan. The team's medic provided the critical logistical coordination. "I woke up and I just said, 'Guys, we have no missions today. I can't make you go, but what do you say we go out to the village, scoop the kid up, and bring him back and have him evaluated?' All my men said, 'Let's go,' and immediately began to don the 50-plus pounds of protective gear and readied the Humvees for another mission."

Later that same day, Larry and his men surrounded the boy's home and staged an "arrest" of the boy and his father. The feigned arrest was necessary to dispel any notion that the father was too friendly with U.S. forces. The soldiers simply wanted to bring the child to the American camp where he could be examined by a physician who was a pediatric cardiologist back home.

A Doppler ultrasound was performed at the camp, and the cardiologist at last had a diagnosis for Ali's father. His son was suffering from a transposition of the great arteries, a condition in which the aorta and pulmonary arteries are reversed, disrupting the supply of oxygen from the heart to the bloodstream. Ali's blood oxygen saturation levels were so low—around 68 percent—that the doctors didn't know how he had lived to be 9 years old. In fact, Ali was so tiny he looked as if he were closer to 5. He suffered from malnutrition because he was sick all of the time and didn't want to eat.

"His father was pleading with us to help him," Larry recalled. "I said, 'If we can help we are going to try and help. But at the end of all of this, the potential cure may kill your son. Do you understand that?' The boy's father said, 'From the second day Ali was born, they told me he had a heart problem. I wanted to find somebody that would at least attempt to cure him. I am ready to accept those risks.' So once I had the dad eye to eye, and we understood each other as dads, I said, 'We'll do what we can.'" Ali's plight had a special poignancy for Larry, who also had a son. "He was a 9-year-old boy, and I had a 9-year-old boy at home," Larry said simply.

Larry e-mailed his colleagues back home, asking if there was any way Larry's Army could help this boy. That e-mail set into motion a chain of events. Two of Larry's colleagues, Rick Sokoler and John Palmer, worked their networks. They raised money from dozens of people, including Major League Baseball players; they involved the Rotary Club; and they enlisted the support of Senator Hillary Clinton's staff to help obtain visas for Ali and his father, Mohammed.

They involved the Ronald McDonald House and convinced a leading surgeon at Albany Medical Center to take the case. They partnered with a U.S.-based Islamic organization to provide translation and spiritual support, and with a travel agent who had experience getting American contractors in and out of Iraq. Every day there was a new challenge and new hope that somehow Larry and his support group would be able to get Ali out of Iraq and into the hands of skilled physicians in the United States.

That day finally came. As Larry described it, "We did a final capture of Ali and his father. We told them, within 24 hours we are going to send for you and hook up with you in a secret place. We are going to give you the tickets, and you have to be at Baghdad Airport. My guys threw money in a hat, and we gave his family about $500. We gave them the tickets, and they were at the airport in Baghdad the next day on their way to Jordan.

"They got to Jordan on July 7, the same day the London bombing happened," Larry continued, "and no visas were being issued—understandably. Rick placed a couple of phone calls, and somehow he got a line into Hillary Clinton's office. We don't know who placed the call, but Ali and his dad were pulled out of line and brought into the embassy and given visas. They were on their way."

"Rick took charge at this point," Larry recalled. "It was at this time that the Iraqi army was tapped to lead a methodical clearing of areas in and around Baghdad, and therefore the 5th Battalion was going to get very busy. We were doing 24-hour operations. At the same time, while we were out on a mission, an Apache helicopter got shot down flying cover for us and the other units in our sector. So we shifted over to a search and capture mission of trying to capture the guys who shot it down. That took 3 weeks of our time, 24 hours, 7 days a week. My Iraqis would not leave until they found the guys."

While Larry was busy in Baghdad, Rick picked up Ali and his father from Kennedy International Airport in New York and took them up to Albany, where the medical team began their evaluations. It turned out that Ali needed extensive dental work and testing before he could be brought into surgery. The boy was finally operated on in late July. Five days after his surgery, Ali went on a walking tour of Albany. He walked farther that day than he had walked in his entire life. Ali's blood oxygen levels are now normal, as is his life expectancy.

Larry Bradley and his unit received Meritorious Service Medals for helping Ali get the medical care that saved his life. Larry's entire unit made it home, every one of them.

If there were ever a legitimate, built-in excuse for not getting involved in someone else's problem, it was available to Larry Bradley.

It would have been completely understandable if he had ignored Ali so as not to get sidetracked from his primary mission. But that's not what happened. At a critical moment, amid everything else that was going on, Larry remained open to considering whether he and his men could help.

Larry Bradley's response falls within a very clear fourth choice along the path, which is consistent across all of our interviewees. He is open to an opportunity. He brings an open mind to an opportunity to help solve a problem beyond his own personal agenda. Like that of our other interviewees, Larry's openness to an opportunity emerges from, and is a natural extension of, the three previous traits discussed. First, Larry leveraged his life experiences, particularly a value taught to him by his father: "Do the right thing." Second, Larry had a clear sense of fairness that allowed him to see the seemingly hopeless plight of a father who was struggling through life in a war-torn part of the world with few resources, much uncertainty, and questionable allies. Third, Larry believed he might be able to make a difference to Ali if he allowed himself to try, as evidenced by the conversation he had with his men. "We went back that night, talked about him, and said what can we do? We threw some ideas around." But at that point, it could have gone either way: do something or do nothing.

The critical distance between doing nothing and doing something is bridged by two closely linked behaviors. First, it's the predisposition to respond in some way that might be part of a solution to a problem at hand. Second, it's the ability to get outside oneself and look at a problem through another person's eyes or from a larger perspective.

## A Predisposition to Respond

A predisposition to respond is an open-minded consideration of the possibilities, rather than an immediate dead end. It is the inclination to say *yes,* let me consider helping or getting involved, rather than the inflexible impasse of the word *no.* Consider the following telephone conversation.

Late on a Friday afternoon, the telephone rang in the office of Holy Family Church, a small parish in Waukegan, Illinois. Father Gary Graf, the pastor of the church, just happened to answer the phone as everyone else had left for the day. The caller said he was Miguel Zavala, a parishioner. Father Gary remembered Miguel as he had performed the wedding ceremony for Miguel's eldest son a few months earlier.

"I remembered Miguel was sick and that he looked very bad at the wedding," Father Gary told us. "I didn't know exactly what he had, but I knew he was pretty much in the process of dying. As I got more into the conversation with him, he described his sickness. He said it was a disease that attacks the liver and that he was in the final stages of cirrhosis. He said there was a possibility of a transplant, and he asked me if we could do a campaign for him in the parish. We had just done a campaign for someone who needed bone marrow, and he asked if we could do something for him. He said he had limited family here, and there were problems with donor compatibility."

Before he hung up the phone with Miguel, Father Gary said he would be happy to conduct a campaign for him in the parish. But then Father Gary said, "Before I ask anyone else to offer themselves as a possible candidate, let me offer myself first. Let me see if I am first compatible."

"That just came out of my mouth," Father Gary recalled. "As soon as that came out of my mouth I immediately knew that this was going to happen. Miguel gave me a phone number, and I called the number that evening. I ended up getting through to a nurse. I told her I just had this conversation with Miguel and that he told me he's a candidate for a transplant. I am calling to get more information. I asked what Miguel's blood type was and they said A positive. I knew that I was A positive. Right then I knew this was going to happen. I told the nurse I was the same blood type as him, and I wanted to offer myself as a candidate. I told absolutely no one else about this, because I knew people would try to talk me out of it."

On a Wednesday morning, April 17, 2002, following the necessary preparations, 60 percent of Father Gary's liver was removed and given to Miguel during a 10-hour surgery at Northwestern Memorial Hospital in Chicago. Miguel, whose liver function had diminished to about 12 percent over a number of years, received 60 percent of a healthy organ immediately. But for Father Gary, the opposite occurred. His body was not prepared for such a drastic change. His liver function went from 100 percent to 40 percent overnight, and his body rebelled. His recovery was slow and painful, but he survived. The life of Miguel Zavala, the 49-year-old father of five children, was saved.

It would have been very easy for Father Gary to avoid becoming a liver donor to Miguel. He was not a family member, and at age 43, Father Gary was at the upper end of the qualifying age limit for a donor. But that was not how Father Gary responded. His predisposition, his immediate response was, "Let me offer myself first."

As Father Gary told us, "It was almost as if my entire life had prepared me to say yes at that moment. Everything I had done previous to that prepared me for this opportunity to be willing and to be able to say yes. At least raise my hand and let me offer. It just seemed like the appropriate thing to do with what was presented to me at that point in my life."

Then, with contemplation and conviction, Father Gary offered a larger perspective: "You are making plans for the future, all the things you want to do in the future that keep you from doing something at the present moment. You've got to do this, you've got to do that. You've got to plan for the future. We know we can't change the past, and the future hasn't come yet. So the only thing we really have is now. Consumed with the present and making the right decision right now, that's all we have. To be able to look at life that way so that when an opportunity presents itself we will be disposed to say yes."

A predisposition to respond also creates possibilities by encouraging constructive problem solving. This was the approach taken by Mike and Tracey Goffman. It was at the end of August 2005, when Hurricane Katrina hit the coast of New Orleans. The Goffmans received a call from Whitney Keller, a tile installer they had met at a trade show in Florida and stayed in touch with over the years. Whitney said his family was okay, but they were scattered. Some were in Tennessee, some were in Florida, and some were in Houston. As the storm continued, the Kellers realized the evacuation wasn't temporary. They lived very close to the 17th Street Canal, the one that all of the television stations covered as the levees broke. They realized they couldn't go home: their house was under a couple feet of water and heavily damaged. They needed a place to stay. The Goffmans offered their help.

"We got the call, and we have 11 people heading north," Tracey recalled. Mike and Tracey live in a three-bedroom house with an unfinished basement in the town of Bristol, Wisconsin, a rural farming community with a population of around 2,000 people. "We started calling our friends," Tracey continued. "People are bringing beds over and blankets so we could set up ahead of time. I was in a business network group, and I called them asking if I could buy some carpet remnants. I told them what we were doing, and they gave us some carpet. We were just scrambling to remodel our basement very quickly—overnight. We carpeted and got beds."

As circumstances developed, Whitney called Mike and Tracey and said that some of his family were being diverted to Houston, but the rest were still heading north. "Whitney made the trip up with them, but didn't stay," Mike said. "He knew they weren't close with us, and he wanted to make sure there was a good transition while taking part of his family and sticking them in our home." Whitney left a few days later.

As it turned out, the Goffmans housed four people—Whitney's brother, Dan; his wife, Kelly; their two children, Katelyn, 8, and Jamie, 3—along with their two dogs for nearly 2 months. Along the way, the Goffmans also housed a friend of the Keller family who had been displaced. Mike and Tracey put Dan to work as a tile setter in their business. They helped get Katelyn in school, and they gave Kelly a car so she could drive the kids around. They passed the hat a few times at their local lodge to get the family some cash. They also made an appeal over the Open Road radio station and collected an additional $1,000.

The Goffmans' Odd Fellows Lodge also began collecting things for the Kellers' return to New Orleans. As Mike told us, "We had a food drive, and we put together a list and put it up at our lodge. On our website we started promoting the items they would need, and we identified a drop off location at our lodge in Richmond, Illinois. We started collecting things in a semitrailer that was parked outside the lodge. We collected everything from bottled water, to bleach, to canned foods, clothes, toys, toiletries, razors, shaving cream, soap, and all of the basics. Those were important things that people needed down there. They ran out of everything. We held a pancake breakfast and a dinner where all of the proceeds went to their family directly. We got them set up with a huge water tank for fresh water, a generator, and extra fuel. Whitney's truck was all ready to take him back to his community. They were able to survive."

We asked Mike and Tracey if they had any apprehension about taking five people in need into their home. They told us they never hesitated. In fact, they never even discussed it. "Our house is like a revolving door," Mike said. "Since we've been married we have not spent 12 months by ourselves in our home. We've always opened up our home. We've always welcomed anyone. We both feel that way."

"Friends and family are very important to me," Tracey added. "I never like to see anyone with hurt feelings or displaced."

One of our most descriptive behaviors is how we respond to an opportunity to be helpful to someone else. If you have ever said to someone, "I have a problem," you know there are two very opposite responses. On the one hand, the person may have responded, "How can I help?" On the other hand, his or her response may have been, "I am sorry to hear that. I hope it works out for you."

An opportunity to make a difference can present itself in many ways. It can come in the form of a sick 9-year-old boy, a needed liver transplant, or an uninvited calamity the size of Hurricane Katrina. As we learned from our interviewees, when presented with an opportunity to help, their first impulse is to respond. They may or may not be able to do anything, but helping is their first consideration. This critical mind-set is the first step in being open to an opportunity—at least considering it, rather than summarily dismissing it at the outset. After all, without a predisposition to respond, not much more can happen.

Furthermore, our interviewees' predisposition to respond is inextricably tied to the beliefs they hold about themselves. Our interviewees know what they are prepared to do because their behavior and choices are guided and driven by clear self-expectations. How do we know? It's a more subtle but consistent measure. We know because when suddenly presented with a problem, their predisposition to respond is neither denied nor confined by the surprise of the moment. They are not rattled or unsettled by the unexpected. Instead, their real-time, in-the-moment openness to an opportunity is preserved by the preparation of knowing what they require of themselves. They may not have expected the opportunity presented to them, but they know what to expect of themselves.

Simply put, they were each prepared to live their belief before being tested to do so. Larry Bradley knew he was prepared to "do the right thing" and helped little Ali. Father Gary Graf was prepared to raise his hand and say, "Let me offer myself first" and helped Miguel. Mike and Tracey Goffman were prepared to "welcome anyone," and reconfigured their home, personally inconvenienced themselves, and stitched together a temporary life for five victims of a natural disaster. They each had a predisposition to respond to a need. They were each open to an opportunity placed before them because their beliefs are self-defining and action oriented. To not respond, or at least weigh the consideration, would have been to deny who they are to themselves. A moment of truth is hard to duck. In the final analysis, dutifully, they act in accordance with their beliefs.

But providence doesn't always drop an opportunity into our lap with the bluntness of an unexpected encounter or a desperate plea or a phone call. For this reason, being open to an opportunity is encouraged not only by a predisposition to respond. As we learned from our interviewees, it also requires a second and equally critical component: the ability to get outside oneself. Our interviewees demonstrate the ability to maintain an external focus. They are attuned to the world around them.

## Get Outside Yourself

We all see it: homelessness. It strikes most of us as unfortunate. It strikes some of us harder than others.

Peter Samuelson started out on his 15-mile (24 kilometer) weekend bicycle ride through Los Angeles. It's not as if he didn't have anything to think about on his personal to-do list. As a Hollywood motion picture and television producer and the founder of the Starlight

Children's Foundation, his to-do list is never empty. But on this particular weekend, something else drew his attention, something outside of his own agenda: the number of homeless people along his route.

"I started counting the homeless people," Peter told us. "I got to 62 in my 15-mile route." As he reflected, "One of the things that worked well for me over the years is that when I am a little bit scared by something, or bothered by it, I sort of force myself to go ahead and do it."

In this case, Peter forced himself to interview the homeless, to speak with them individually. "One of the things I made myself do was actually to look at them in the eyes, which I think was a shocking experience for them because most people don't do that," he explained. "Even when there is someone panhandling, and you give them money, I think you try not to look the guy in the face. I made myself do that. Of course, that immediately makes a one-on-one thing that lifts the relationship into a different place.

"I didn't say I would interview all 62 in the first go-around," Peter commented. "I did one, and then I did five, and then I did 15, and then I did all 62." Peter was trying to discover the answer to two questions. "One of the things I asked them was, 'Tell me, first of all, where do you get money so you can buy food and other things?' I also asked them, 'Where do you sleep at night?'"

Peter told us he discovered from his interviews that about half of the homeless panhandle, and the other half recycle. "At night, it turns out that there are 75,000 homeless people in Los Angeles, but there are only 12,500 beds for them. This means on any given night there are around 62,500 people—human beings—about 60 percent male, 40 percent female, and 18 percent children under the age of 18, who are sleeping in cardboard boxes, behind a dumpster, under the freeway overpass, or on a piece of concrete. I got really frustrated with that. It was absurd. Mostly, what they use in the daytime for the recycling side is an obviously stolen shopping cart because it has four wheels, and you can put your stuff inside and push it around."

With his new insights into the routines and needs of the homeless, Peter went to the Art Center College of Design in Pasadena and met with the dean. Peter put up some prize money for an object—a three-dimensional object—that he called, but without much more definition, an EDAR—Everyone Deserves a Roof. Peter told us that the graduate students at the college designed an amazing array of EDARS. He met two design students, Eric Lindeman and Jason Zasa. Peter took their model prototype and found the largest manufacturer of shopping carts west of the Mississippi, a company called Precision Wire. He met with them, and they volunteered to do a computer-aided design, as well as the fabrication of a series of prototypes.

Peter described the EDAR: "It is this thing, which in the daytime looks a bit like a shopping cart but with a top on it. The glory of it is that in the daytime you use it for your recycling, but at night the whole thing unhinges and folds out with a cover. It becomes a single-person tent that is off the ground and is reasonably comfortable with a very robust metal frame. We have a tent manufacturer that is working on the cover. It obviously has to be waterproof, windproof, and nonflammable. We have around 300 of them on the streets now with a *www.edar.org* on the side. We give the homeless clients a number to dial and tell us what broke, what was good, what was bad, and we've learned from that. The goal is to make a very serious dent in getting those 62,500 people in the greater Los Angeles area up off the concrete and out of the wet."

As it turned out, Peter Samuelson's curiosity during his weekend bicycle ride morphed into something very tangible. On March 9, 2009, CNN televised the results of Peter's efforts. At a cost of $500 each, 60 homeless people were by then testing EDAR on the streets of Los Angeles. Affectionately referred to by its occupants as the "Hobo Condo," it is one possible alternative for 80 percent of the urban homeless in the United States for whom no shelter bed is available. As Peter said, "It is not perfect. Apartments would be much better. On a 10 scale, it is a 5. But for 62,500 people in just one city, they have a zero."

The simplest and easiest way to avoid an opportunity is to not pay attention to the world around us. But our interviewees do pay attention. Peter put the problems of the homeless front and center for himself. He could have kept riding his bike with well-disciplined blinders that make the visible invisible.

But Peter Samuelson opted for close encounters with homelessness in order to strip down its pervasiveness, its intensity, its hopelessness.

He sought out the ultraneedy. Most of us spend our lives distancing ourselves from them. Peter, on the other hand, wanted to understand the facts from their perspective. He looked in their eyes and interviewed them one-on-one. For Peter, humanity was not an abstraction to be contemplated. He found humanity in the faces of individuals. And, putting his empathy into action, he found an alternative solution to a problem. In short, Peter Samuelson did exactly what the pioneering social psychologist Kurt Lewin advised when he said that the best way to truly understand something is to try to change it.[1]

It's not always easy to get outside of ourselves, especially when our personal needs are compelling. But it is possible to do so. Consider Kathryn Funderburk and her resolve to focus her attention on the needs of others.

Kathryn was born with cystic fibrosis. She has severe difficulty breathing, as well as complications with digestion. She has an intense daily routine that includes nebulizers to clear her lungs and physical therapy. By the time she reached 14, the cystic fibrosis had created a companion disease: insulin dependent diabetes. But her challenges have not prevented her from seeing the difficulties of others.

During high school, Kathryn volunteered at a homeless shelter where she cooked and served meals. She donated her time to the Braintree Buddies Program, which assists students with special needs by taking them to the shopping mall, helping them make purchases, and counting out change. She has been involved in fundraisers for various causes, including serving the needs of a local group in Mexico. As a member of the National Honor Society, she tutored other students and helped with the recycling program at school. As a college student at Harvard, she continued her efforts by teaching English as a second language on Saturday mornings for several years.

It all begins with Kathryn's focus on other people. Her predisposition toward helping those who experience life's difficulties is best seen in the description of her work at the homeless shelter. "After we were done cooking and serving, we would sit down and eat with the men at the homeless shelter and have conversations with them. There would not be a separation between us. These are real people. Some of them didn't have a family, but others did. Some would talk about their children and grandchildren. We like to lump certain groups of people together: the homeless, the mentally ill, and certain racial and religious groups. We do this out of necessity sometimes, but each individual has their own individual stories."

From birth, we are wired for self-preservation. It's the evolutionary imprint for taking care of ourselves. The British philosopher Herbert Spencer even gave it a name that was popularized by Charles Darwin: survival of the fittest. But self-preservation doesn't necessarily mean we act selfishly. Some social scientists are now positing that our tendency to help others is exactly what has enabled us to survive as a species. Sometimes called "the survival of the kindest," this interpretation of Darwin's theory of evolution by natural selection suggests that human beings have survived because we have evolved the capacity to cooperate and care for those in need, including our very vulnerable young. Some of the most important work on this subject is being carried out at the University of California, Berkeley, by Dacher Keltner, a psychologist and author of *Born to Be Good: The Science of a Meaningful Life*, and a team of social scientists. Keltner notes that Darwin, writing almost 130 years ago, elevated sympathy to "our strongest passion."[2]

Thus, it's not surprising that Kathryn Funderburk is able to step outside her own daily routine of critical needs, beyond self-absorption and preoccupation with personal concerns. Getting outside of herself prepares her to be open to opportunities to help others. Kathryn Funderburk and Peter Samuelson grasp what all of our interviewees understand: We cannot know what is outside of us if we only have an internal view.

Life isn't tidy. It's often messy. Opportunities present themselves to us on their own schedule—in the middle of a battlefield, a randomly answered phone call, during a weekend bike ride, or requests for volunteers at school. It's important to see what is capable of crossing our path on any given day.

As we learned from our interviewees, being open to an opportunity to make a difference appears to emerge from a predisposition to respond and an external focus. Their predisposition to respond is driven by their beliefs about themselves, echoing once again that an understanding of others is deeper if preceded by an understanding of self. Their external focus allows them to step outside of themselves and focus on the world around them.

The paradox, if there is one, lies in how the strength of a belief is not always reflected in behavior. Many of us believe hunger is wrong or unfair, but how many of us do something about it? For our interviewees, however, their self-beliefs drive their behavior because they serve as standards for conducting their lives.

Rather than sifting through a lot of incoherent rationalizations, each interviewee in his or her own way was guided by a fundamental question: Am I acting like my best self in accordance with my beliefs? Somewhere along the abbreviated arc of reasoning, there was no moral puzzle to solve, no confusion of values, no intellectual straight-jacket to wrestle. The inner debate was crisp and uncomplicated because their beliefs are simple and straightforward guidelines for conducting their lives.

The beliefs they hold about themselves help them focus on being—in the form of constantly becoming—the person they expect themselves to be. In this regard, they each knew their response to the opportunity presented to them would be an authentic self-assessment of who they are. Soldier, priest, married couple, movie producer, or student, they know a sense of responsibility is not what you are, it's who you are—first to yourself and then to the world around you.

When faced with an opportunity to make a difference, Larry Bradley, Father Gary Graf, Mike and Tracey Goffman, Peter Samuelson, and Kathryn Funderburk all knew what they expected of themselves. They were predisposed to respond long before they were confronted with an opportunity to make a difference because they each knew their belief and what it required them to do.

Somewhere, deep inside the gray folds of our thinking, where contradictions between our beliefs and behaviors coexist, it's important to clarify the standard by which we want to live our lives. Our interviewees construct such a standard by deconstructing their lives first. They have clarity about a few fundamental questions worth pondering.

- Do I believe I am someone who invites or avoids responsibility?
- What should I expect of myself when confronted with an opportunity to help someone?
- Am I aware of the needs around me or am I overly self-absorbed?

Until we clarify such self-expectations, our predisposition to respond to a need outside our own personal agenda is less likely to emerge.[3] Our beliefs do not have to be specific, only directional. When confronted with an opportunity to make a difference, what will be your impulse? What would you be inclined to do? It all begins with what we believe to be true about ourselves when presented with an opportunity. We are then faced with the next choice along the path, taking the first small step.

## How Will You Respond to Someone in Need?

1. Major Larry Bradley came across his helping opportunity quite unexpectedly when his unit in Iraq encountered Ali, a young local boy with critical breathing difficulties. Larry's life experiences and training had prepared him to respond by helping. How would you respond in a similar situation? Do you think Larry should have helped Ali, or should he have focused on his primary mission in Iraq? Do you think helping Ali served a larger purpose?

2. Father Gary Graf, who donated part of his liver to save the life of a parishioner, observed that sometimes "all the things you want to do in the future keep you from doing something in the present moment." How might this statement apply to you? Think about how you have spent the past day, the past week, the past month. How much of your thought and activity were directed to the future instead of the present? How would being more mindful of the present allow you to experience life more fully? How does being more present in the moment contribute to a predisposition to respond to those in need?

3. Sometimes, like Peter Samuelson, who decided to help the homeless in Los Angeles, or Kathryn Funderburk, who has given countless hours of volunteer service despite her own battle with cystic fibrosis, helping others involves getting outside of one's own world and seeing the needs of others. Helping others often involves sacrificing one's own immediate needs to help someone else. Can you think of a time when you stepped outside of your world and came face to face with

someone in need? Was this encounter difficult in any way? What did you learn from it?

4. Sometimes there is a troubling disparity between one's own beliefs about the right thing to do and one's actions. Is there an instance in your experience when you struggled with this disparity, and if so, how did you resolve it? Do you have a standard by which you conduct yourself in the face of someone in need?

5. A predisposition to respond involves a willingness to problem solve in order to help people in need. We saw this in the stories of both Larry Bradley and Mike and Tracey Goffman. Can you think of a time when you were called on to help someone in need and you responded by constructive problem solving, perhaps marshaling the involvement of others as well?

6. A growing body of research challenges the traditional belief that we are wired to be selfish in order to survive—the "every man for himself" interpretation of Darwin. The more recent "survival of the kindest" thinking suggests that we are evolving to be more compassionate and collaborative to ensure survival. What light does this newer thinking shed on the altruistic actions of the people in this book?

# Part Three

## Making A Difference

*I shall be telling this with a sigh*

*Somewhere ages and ages hence.*

*Two roads diverged in a wood, and I—*

*I took the one less traveled by,*

*And that has made all the difference.*

—Robert Frost, "The Road Not Taken"

# 5

# Taking the First Small Step

## *A Seventh Grade Speech*

C raig Kielburger is a world leader. Not as head of a government, but as an individual who has profoundly impacted the lives of millions of people, mostly children, all over the world. He has received numerous international awards and accolades, including nine honorary doctorate degrees and the Roosevelt Freedom Medal. He is one of the youngest recipients of the Order of Canada. With his brother, Marc, he has authored a best-selling book, *Me to We*.

Craig is the founder of Free The Children. The organization has built more than 650 schools and schoolrooms around the world, offering more than 55,000 children access to education. It has helped 30,000 women and men achieve economic self-sufficiency through micro loans and alternative income programs and has created clean water, sanitation, and health care projects that have benefited over 1 million people. Free The Children also sponsors programs in North America and the United Kingdom that provide more than a million young people with the tools and know-how to take action on social issues. At this writing, Craig is 28 years old.

We could literally devote an entire book to Craig's leadership. The initiatives that have grown from his leadership are many and varied, and include an innovative social enterprise called Me to We that donates half its net profits to Free The Children. Support from Me to We means that a greater percentage of charitable donations can go directly to humanitarian projects, rather than administrative costs. Among other programs, Me to We sells crafts made by artisans in local countries, runs summer leadership academies, and takes 1,300 students a year overseas on volunteer trips.

The leadership lessons we learn from Craig Kielburger, however, come not so much from admiring his accomplishments, though they are certainly admirable. The lessons are in better understanding where all this rippling, snowballing energy started; in other words, how he came to take the first small step—the fifth choice along the path. For that understanding, we let Craig tell his own story.

"I was 12 when Free The Children first started because of a newspaper article that I read. I was looking through the comics at the time. Every morning I would flip through the paper, the *Toronto Star*. On the bottom of the front page, there is a little index box that tells you where your horoscope, the comics, etc., are. I turned over the paper looking for this box on the front page, and there was this picture of a young boy, Iqbal Masih, with his bright red vest and his fist clenched. His arm was high in the air, and the headlines said, 'Battled Child Labor,' underneath it 'Boy Twelve,' and underneath that, 'Murdered.'

"Because I was 12, I started reading this article about the life of this young boy who grew up in the outskirts of Lahore, Pakistan," Craig continued. "Lahore is a large city in Pakistan, and he grew up in the rural areas. He was sold at the age of 4 into slavery, bonded labor. He worked in a carpet factory. He escaped when he was 10 and started speaking out against child labor and became quite prominent. He even spoke in the United States, in Boston. Around the world his story was spread, and when he was 12 he returned to Pakistan, and he was shot dead outside of his house. He was assassinated."

As we saw earlier when we talked about making a connection, Craig felt an immediate bond with this young boy who lived halfway around the world. "Nothing ever connected with me or just hit me emotionally as hard as it did reading this story," Craig told us. "I think it was because we were exactly the same age. Even though we were a world apart, two very different lives, that slight bond connected us. I could imagine myself in his position and feeling so incredibly angry. Why him? Why not me? Why me here? Why him there?"

Craig was so angry that he tore off the front page of the paper, shoved it into his backpack, and brought it to school that day. "I remember riding the school bus and constantly looking at it and thinking that I wanted to do something to help. I had no idea what. A lot of what I thought about was my brother. I remembered how when he was about the same age he had started this campaign to try to help the environment. I still have this image in my mind of my brother because I believed in him, so I believed in myself. I thought, well, he did it; therefore, I could do it.[1]

"So I got to my grade 7 class. I had a speech impediment when I was younger, so speaking in front of people was absolutely terrifying," Craig said. "I'm still uncomfortable, but back then it was completely petrifying. But I stood up in front of my class and just read this article, and I said, 'I need your help, who will join?' There were 11 hands. Eleven friends put up their hands and that is how Free The Children first started, with my grade 7 class.

"Well, the next step was actually to call other organizations," Craig continued. "Originally, we didn't set out to start an organization. We just wanted to join with someone already active. No one took us seriously because we were all kids. One group actually said if we wanted to help we could bring our parents' credit cards. So we started our own group. We didn't have a name. We just called ourselves the Group of 12. We did car washes, bake sales, pop bottle drives, we started a petition. We were giving talks at local schools because we realized that if adults wouldn't take us seriously then we would turn to those who would—which was the young people."

As remarkable as this story is, it contains an element that is absolutely present, in one form or another, in the narrative of every one of the 31 people we interviewed for this book: a pivotal moment when leadership emerges. Every story of leadership—taking charge of a problem or challenging situation with initiative, energy, and a commitment to make a difference—contains such a defining moment. It is a point in time when an impulse is followed, a small step is taken, and action occurs that at that point cannot possibly be understood, even by those present and involved, in terms of where it will lead.

This must have been the case when Rosa Parks refused to give up her seat on the bus to a white man in segregated Montgomery, Alabama, in 1955. And something similar must have happened when Martin Luther King, Jr., first heard of Rosa Parks's act of defiance and wondered whether he should go and see if he could help out.

We believe that leadership is too often examined as something that occurs in moments of great drama, with the world as its stage, media scurrying and floodlights glaring. We have been reminded, through this research, that leadership often occurs in relatively lonely moments, in small acts of great courage.[2]

One of those moments of courage also occurred in the life of Ryan Hreljac, who, you may recall, started an organization called Ryan's Well Foundation. Since its inception in 2001, this organization has helped provide clean water and improved sanitation for nearly three-quarters of a million people. Although he launched an organization that today reaches around the globe, Ryan's critical moment of aware-ness arrived when he was just 6 years old, in his first grade classroom. The class was discussing how they could raise money for projects in developing countries.

As we saw earlier, Ryan's teacher explained to the students that millions of people in the world had to walk long distances to get clean water, while more fortunate people, like Ryan and his classmates, only had to take a few steps to the nearest drinking fountain. This realization was as powerful for Ryan as the face of the murdered Pakistani boy in the newspaper was for Craig, and he felt a similar compulsion to do something about it.

At first, Ryan took the small step of doing extra chores around the house to raise the $70 his teacher had told him would pay for a well. When he eventually found out that a well would cost closer to $2,000, he knew he couldn't raise the money alone. With his parents' encour-agement, Ryan began looking for alternatives. "I spoke to our local Rotary Club. Then there was a little thing in the newspaper, and there was a little TV interview," he told us. "And then I spoke to a school. Slowly it grew and grew. Don't get me wrong. I still came home at the end of the day and played with my toys and hung out with my friends. It was just sort of a school project. It's still a school project; it just never really ended."

Both of these stories involve very young people, and they illustrate the fact that leadership can emerge at a relatively young age. But it need not, and often does not, emerge this early. Most of the people you have already encountered in this book took their first leadership steps at later points in life. And though age is not a deciding factor, perhaps not even an important factor in understanding the emergence of leadership, two patterns are present in our interviewees that occur with such consistency that they deserve special attention: taking a bite-size perspective and adopting a positive attitude.

## Bite-Size Perspective

One of the more surprising conclusions we've reached from talking to our interviewees is that when they think about a social problem or issue, they tend to think in relatively small terms. That is, they typically do not go through all the rationalizations and excuse-making that allow most of us to distance ourselves from the pressing social problems all around us. We have already discussed many of these rationalizations in Chapter 3, some of those ways we have of talking to ourselves that allow us to see issues or problems as so overwhelming, so long-standing, so impossible to impact that the only reasonable course of action is to do nothing. Leaders, on the other hand, tend to talk to themselves more about what can be done, what is possible. This different, bite-size perspective is present consistently throughout our interviewees.

Lucy Helm, whose full-time job is senior vice president and deputy general counsel at Starbucks Coffee Company, finds time every summer to spend a week as codirector of Camp Parkview, a residential camp for developmentally challenged adults on Vashon Island in Washington state. The camp offers traditional activities like swimming, boating, archery, and arts and crafts for developmentally challenged people and a respite for their parents or guardians, who often need a break from relentless caregiving. Lucy, who began volunteering with people with disabilities as a counterpoint to the pressures of law school, isn't looking to solve the often intractable problems of people with disabilities. She finds just making a human connection satisfying and meaningful.

"People with developmental disabilities are often isolated because I think people are either too scared or intimidated and don't know how to take the first step of interacting with people with disabilities," Lucy told us. She has made a difference by taking the seemingly small step of looking beyond the stereotypes to see the humanity of those with mental disabilities. "You realize that they are just people like you," Lucy said. "Just being able to relate is what's important. I think when you have genuine relationships with people with any kind of disability, that what they appreciate the most is being treated like you would treat anyone else." Lucy added, "Where I get humbled by it is the pure essence of humanity that you're getting to experience."

Think back, too, to a couple of other people we've already introduced you to, Inderjit Khurana and Jennifer Atler. Inderjit, you will recall, was the remarkable teacher in India who received awards from other nations for creating schools on India's railway platforms that enrich the lives of the country's homeless and indigent children. What is notable here is the relatively modest way in which Inderjit began. As we saw earlier, Inderjit started a small preschool for local children in Bhubaneswar whose parents could pay a nominal fee. She was distressed, however, to see the half-naked and dirty children who lingered outside the school's gates.

Guided by the simple idea that "if the child cannot come to a school, take the school to the child," Inderjit decided to take the first small step to help change their lives. Along with a colleague, she began by bringing the tools of learning to the railway stations—books, paper, crayons—along with soap to allow the children to bathe. Although today Inderjit's Ruchika organization sponsors schools in numerous railway stations and runs other programs to help the dispossessed in India, her original goal was far more modest. She wanted poor children to experience some of the pleasures of childhood that her own children enjoyed. "Even if I can transform their lives for 2 hours a day, then I give them back a childhood full of fun and freedom, and they know that somebody cares," Inderjit said.

Jennifer Atler, we learned earlier, was the executive director of Invest in Kids, an unusually successful citizens group in Colorado that searches for and evaluates evidence-based programs that enhance the quality of life for children and their families, and then helps communities adopt and manage these programs. Although Jennifer is a recognized and established leader now, she tells a somewhat different story about her beginning. "I was a corporate attorney at Holland & Hart, and there was a senior partner there who knew that my passion was really working with kids, and he was representing a lot of different nonprofits pro bono around the community," Jennifer told us. "So he took me along to his nonprofit clients, and one of them was this group of attorneys who were about to form Invest in Kids. It was all partners from firms around town and me, and I was a first-year associate fresh out of law school, so I rarely spoke in the meetings. But at the end, whenever there was something to do to follow up, to get the work done for the next meeting, I always volunteered to do that." From that first tentative step of offering to help in whatever way she could, Jennifer grew in confidence and competence until she finally left her law firm to help found and eventually become the executive director of Invest in Kids.

This is the pattern that has emerged from our interviews.

• An incredibly important threshold must be crossed in order for leadership to occur. This threshold is the line between inactivity and action. It represents a change in the state of the individualized system, from off to on, from doing nothing to doing something, with respect to a consciously recognized social issue. This action orientation has been found in virtually every analysis of leadership in recent years.[3]

• This threshold may be less of a barrier if people talk to themselves less about why the problem is overwhelming and therefore the barrier is impregnable and more about what can be done and how easy it is to get started.

• Our interviewees don't seem to be thinking intentionally about grand goals or ultimate-end states. They don't seem to be particularly concerned or knowledgeable about where their course of action might ultimately lead. Rather, they seem to be acting from a deep sense of connection and caring for others, and often take a first step that is "natural" or the "only" thing to be done.[4]

• Finally, though an initial act of leadership is typically small and often tentative, it is huge in its implications. It is the distinguishing feature of leadership, the difference between leaders and nonleaders. Most of our interviewees were very explicit about the fact that their lives changed significantly at the point that they made the connection, made the commitment, or took the first step.

The willingness to act, to try, is crucial in any leadership context. Franklin D. Roosevelt, then governor of New York, advised a commencement audience at Oglethorpe University in 1932, during the Great Depression, "It is common sense to take a method and try it. If it fails, admit it frankly and try another. But above all, try something." More colloquially, hockey great Wayne Gretzky is credited with the following straightforward wisdom: "You miss 100 percent of the shots you never take."

## Attitude Is Everything

If we look for some common qualities that will help explain the emergence of our interviewees as leaders; that is, whether they take the first small step, we won't find any of the usual characteristics often recorded on job application forms. Not education, nor training, nor job experience, nor any of the many other indicators of how much we know or how smart we are. And the standard demographics that are usually considered important individual attributes are of relatively little use in explaining why these individuals cross the threshold that separates leaders from the might-have-been. Age doesn't seem to account for much. Nor does gender. Personal wealth seems insignificant. Even ethnicity and culture do not erode the fundamental consistency among our interviewees. Though they varied greatly on the usual standards of comparison, they were remarkably similar in terms of their attitudes.

The most obvious quality in the attitudes displayed by our interviewees and the quality that constantly recurs when you talk with them is "positive." They are optimistic rather than cynical. They look for and dwell on the possibilities, the redeeming qualities in others, the dreams we have in common, the untapped potential in themselves and others. They think of many possible pathways to success and do not obsess over failure. They are confident, though typically humble; they believe in themselves and see inherent value in others.

Since this quality appears so consistently across all of our interviewees, it's difficult to single out only a few people who exemplify it. But a few examples do show the different aspects of what constitutes a positive attitude. Liz Clibourne, "Mama Liz," who brings her medical expertise to Tanzanian villages, welcomes the new challenges that each day brings. "You get up in the morning, boil some water, make your coffee, and you sit on the steps, and the kids come around. You know what you're going to do with your day. Even if you are not sure, the kids will present something. There is always something new happening, and the problems are new problems, and because you are not so constrained with a million rules, you can deal with them."

Peter Samuelson, the movie producer who started the Starlight Children's Foundation, has a profound belief in the goodness of people. "I think most people are inherently decent and faced with a system for expressing their decency, they do it," Peter said. "Both secular and faith-based, I think most people have some kind of moral code."

Gerry Sieck, the corporate lawyer who became a teacher in inner-city Chicago, believes in his ability to make a difference and in the promise of his young students. In Chapter 3, he described teaching as not only the hardest job he's ever had, but also the best job. He told us he found teaching so rewarding because it gave him the chance to see young people test their intellectual boundaries and make constant breakthroughs.

Finally, Dr. Jane Aronson, the infectious diseases specialist who created the Worldwide Orphans Foundation, articulated a very positive vision for the children her organization helps. "My goal is for the kids we serve abroad, regardless of their parental status, for us to provide them with an education and an outlook, a vantage point in life, so they can dream and be anything they want to be." She added that she wants them to have the same advantages her own children have. "I want their hair washed and combed; I want them dressed nicely; I want them to feel good about themselves when they look in the mirror. A lot of my vision is about how children around the world have the right to live a good life."

This combination of qualities one could describe collectively as a positive attitude is the most apparent consistency across these 31 individuals. It's there at the beginning and never goes away. They are living proof of the assertion that a belief that is held true is true in its consequences.[5] That is, leaders who demonstrate a positive attitude impose their will on the world by believing it is possible to do so. They shape the social reality by the way they think about it.

When it comes to leadership, attitude is everything. At the broadest level, the attitude we first encountered in our interviewees was one most of us think of as positive. It is the primary determinant of whether the first step is taken. It is taking this critical first step, the point at which leadership emerges, that we explored in this chapter. In Chapter 7, we look at the full expression of leadership in the leading of others. But first, in Chapter 6, we explore the next choice along the path, perseverance, that crucial quality that determines whether an individual will stay the course when hardships and obstacles arise.

## Taking Your First Leadership Step

1. Craig Kielburger and Ryan Hreljac took their first step toward leadership in what we call a small act of great courage. We noted that, at the time, they probably had no idea where this first act would lead. Can you think of other individuals who began their humanitarian efforts in a similar way? Why do we call this first step an act of courage?

2. Many of the people interviewed for this book began their work in a small way. So often we are told to think big. What are the advantages of sometimes thinking small? Can you think of a time when you did something small—perhaps it even seemed insignificant to you— only to find out that it made a big difference to the person you helped? Can you think of something you might do now, something small to you, that could make a big difference to the other person?

3. We concluded that the single quality that best explains the emergence of leadership among our interviewees is a positive attitude. Why is this quality so important to the success of an effort? Have you worked with leaders who displayed this attitude? How did it influence you? Have you ever worked with a leader who had the opposite attitude? What was the impact of this attitude? Is a positive attitude something that a person can work to develop, or is it part of one's personality?

Dr. Irving Williams examines a child in the Meatu District, Shinyanga Region, Tanzania.

Dr. Irving Williams presents an ambulance to
the Kisarawe District Hospital, Coast Region, Tanzania.

Ali, 9 years old, on the day Army Major Larry Bradley
and his team met him and his father in Iraq

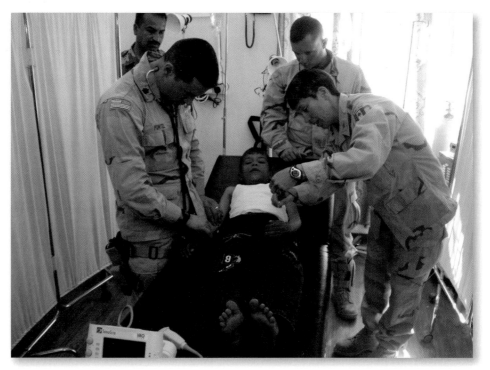

Ali being examined by a pediatric cardiologist during the Easter Sunday mission

Army Major Larry Bradley (front row, far left) with his fellow soldiers in Iraq

Bill Sergeant, a long-time leader in Rotary International's worldwide effort to eradicate polio, stands before a statue erected in his honor in Knoxville, Tennessee.

Teacher Kathryn Funderburk helping a student with a math lesson

Kathryn Funderburk, a teacher at City on a Hill Charter
Public School in the Roxbury neighborhood of Boston

Cheryl Perera speaking out against the commercial sexual exploitation of children

Jennifer Atler, former executive director of Invest in Kids,
with her mother, Marilyn Van Derbur, Miss America, 1958

Ryan Hreljac, 16, with local children at a well in Lira district in Uganda

Craig Kielburger (left), founder of Free The Children,
with his brother, Marc, and children in Kenya

Craig Kielburger with a new friend in Kenya

Pediatrician Jane Aronson, of the Worldwide Orphans
Foundation, on a mission to help children in need in Haiti

Dave Ulrich (right), a University of Michigan business professor, with his wife,
Wendy, and two young missionaries during a 3-year mission with his church to Quebec

Makenzie Snyder packing duffel bags with stuffed animals for foster children

Dr. David J. Winchester with his operating room team in Beijing:
nurses from the Chicago area, who also traveled to Russia and
Latvia with him, and, in green, a Chinese medical professional

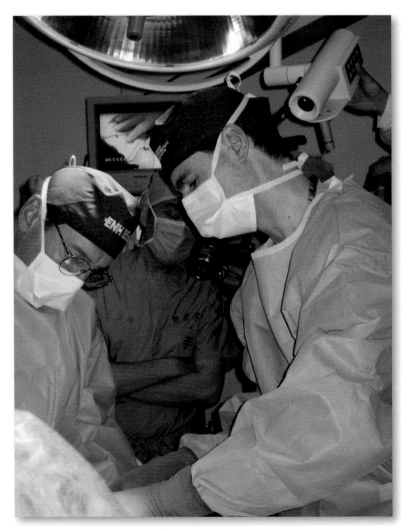

Dr. David J. Winchester (right) and Dr. Stephen Sener, performing and teaching lifesaving procedures during a trip to Beijing, a newer location for the team

Father Gary Graf, liver donor to a parishioner in Waukegan, Illinois

Lucy Helm (left) with fellow Camp Parkview counselors in Washington state

Gerry Sieck, corporate lawyer turned
middle school teacher in inner-city Chicago

Kathy Giusti with daughter, Nicole, and son, David

Kathy Giusti, CEO of the Multiple Myeloma Research Foundation

Sanphasit Koompraphant, a tireless leader against the exploitation and abuse of children in Thailand and the Mekong region

Harry Leibowitz, founder of World of
Children, with a young boy in Ethiopia

Harry Leibowitz with a young girl in Haiti

Inderjit Khurana teaching street children using
a rickshaw converted into a mobile school

Victor Dukay and a staff member with an orphan living
at the Godfrey's Children Center in Idweli, Tanzania

Sherri Kirkpatrick, a nurse, with "Little Boss Mirriam,"
one of the many children Sherri's work has benefited

Sherri Kirkpatrick, a nurse, with health workers in Zambia

Peter Samuelson with an EDAR mobile housing unit, used by homeless people in Los Angeles and a growing number of cities

Liz Clibourne (left), a nurse and teacher, in Kyela, Tanzania, with colleagues

Kathy Magee and Howard Unger, COO of Operation Smile, greet the babies during the opening of the new Operation Smile Charity Care Hospital in Hangzhou, China

Young patients with Clinical Coordinator Norrie Olekers (left) and Bill and Kathy Magee at the Diocesan Caritas Clinic in Barinas, Venezuela

Hui-jung Chi (second from left) at the V shop, a starting
point at the end of sexual violence that offers multiple
employment services for women helped by the Garden of Hope

Hui-jung Chi (center), chief executive of the Garden of Hope, a powerful advocate
for social justice and a voice for the rights of women and children in Taiwan

Margaret Vernon in Rwanda, where she lives and
works following her service in the Peace Corps

Rob Taylor with local residents in Tijuana, Mexico,
where he traveled to help build affordable homes

Rob Taylor (far right) with local residents and fellow volunteers in Tijuana, Mexico

Meg Campbell, executive director, with Thabiti Brown, principal,
Codman Academy Charter Public School, Dorchester, Massachusetts

Mike and Tracey Goffman (front, center) enjoying a night out
with Whitney and Lisa Keller (far left); Dan and Kelly Keller (far right),
who stayed with Mike and Tracey after Hurricane Katrina struck; and friends

A New Orleans neighborhood near the Keller home that
was devastated by Hurricane Katrina, August 2005

Susie Scott Krabacher with one of the tens of
thousands of children she has helped in Haiti

Victor Dukay with an orphan in Tanzania

# 6

# Perseverance

## *These Are the Cards That Were Dealt Me*

Kathy Giusti was 37 years old, a successful pharmaceutical executive and mother of a 1-year-old daughter, when a routine blood test before she was to start fertility treatment changed her life forever. "I remember I got the diagnosis as I was driving in my car and talking to the doctor," Kathy told us. "He was hedging and saying, 'You know you need to come see me personally.' Finally, I said, 'Look, my dad was a doctor. I know this is bad news, so just tell me.' He then proceeded to tell me, while I was in my car, that I had multiple myeloma."

At the time, little was known about the disease. Kathy's doctor could only tell her that multiple myeloma was a form of cancer, and a bone marrow transplant was a possible treatment. In those early days of the Internet before medical information was readily available, Kathy hurried to the bookstore along with her husband, Paul, and pored through all the medical books she could find on the subject. By the time the couple arrived for Kathy's doctor's appointment the next day, she knew to ask about the cancer's staging, in other words, how advanced it was. She had already learned that the disease was inevitably fatal.

Multiple myeloma is a rare cancer of the plasma cells. These cells play an important role in the functioning of the body's immune system, producing antibodies that help fight infection and disease. When plasma cells become malignant, they travel through the bloodstream, eventually collecting in the bone marrow where they cause devastating damage to healthy tissue. In 1996, when Kathy was diagnosed, the outlook for patients with multiple myeloma was grim, with most living only 3 or 4 years.

Because myeloma has no known cure, patients often have the option of delaying aggressive treatment, which is the choice Kathy made. "You want to buy as much time upfront as possible," Kathy explained. She used that time to return to work at the pharmaceutical company Searle, which had been supportive of her medical needs, and to pursue her quest to have a second child. "Because I'm a twin, I've always had somebody by my side," Kathy told us. "I swore if it was the last thing I did and if I died doing it, I was going to have another child—for my daughter, Nicole, for my husband, who is just an unbelievable father, and for me as well." While the in vitro fertilization didn't work at first, eventually it was successful, and Kathy gave birth to a son, David, in 1997. "My life changed the day he was born," Kathy said. "That to me was just a signal that good things were going to happen, and my life was going to turn around a little bit here, and I was just so grateful."

While Kathy was pursuing the parallel paths of fertility and cancer treatment, she discovered something troubling about research into multiple myeloma. Researchers in different parts of the country didn't seem to be talking with one another; they weren't sharing data and findings in a way that could lead to new treatments and maybe even a cure. What's more, few research dollars were even going to the disease.

"Now I understand a lot of what's going on, but it took me many years to figure it out," Kathy said. "Now I can look back and say, I'm not surprised at all there weren't many people working in myeloma. Part of it is because there was no funding for myeloma, and the researchers follow the money trail. There was no glamour or recognition in the disease, and anyone who was working on it was doing it in a silo fashion." Kathy explained that the rewards system in academic medicine is "broken." Researchers are rewarded for individual effort, not for the collaboration that is more likely to yield concrete results for patients, particularly with a rare disease like multiple myeloma.

"I started realizing very early on that I had to do something," Kathy continued. "I remember saying to my sister, 'Money can't buy you time, but maybe it can.' I said to her maybe if we were able to start raising money to fund some of these research ideas—things my own doctor was throwing at me, like what if we did this vaccine. All these things were way out there, but I kept hoping that maybe there was something here."

Kathy's drive to "do something" led to the founding in 1998, along with her twin sister, Karen Andrews, of the Multiple Myeloma Research Foundation (MMRF). The sisters were uniquely qualified to start a groundbreaking charitable organization. Kathy is a graduate of the Harvard Business School with years of managerial experience in the health care field, and her sister is a lawyer. Beyond that, they were motivated to do anything they could to prolong Kathy's life. "I've always been driven," Kathy told us. "I didn't spend a lot of time just sitting there saying, 'Oh my gosh, I'm so sad.' I said, 'These are the cards that were dealt me, and I have to figure out the best way to work with this.'"

Kathy also had a deeply emotional reason to search for a treatment: She wanted to live long enough for her daughter to remember her and to know that she had battled to stay alive. "When I was first diagnosed, I remember calling one of my dear friends who had lost her mother when she was a teenager to cancer. I asked her what she wished her mom had done differently, and she told me that she wished her mom had fought harder." Kathy voiced a more modest wish, as well, "I desperately wanted my daughter to have some vague memory of me."

In addition to MMRF, whose mission is to break down the barriers that slow drug and research development and accelerate the delivery of treatment to patients, Kathy and Karen also created a consortium to foster collaboration among multiple myeloma researchers. The consortium now includes 16 academic centers that conduct clinical trials of next-generation treatments. Kathy runs the foundation like a for-profit business, with an emphasis on accountability and results, and her approach has paid off. MMRF has raised more than $165 million for myeloma-specific research to date. It has contributed to FDA approval of four promising new drugs for multiple myeloma in just 4 years, thereby extending the lives of thousands of patients, including Kathy. In recognition of her achievements, Kathy was named to *Time* magazine's 2011 list of the 100 most influential people in the world.

None of this has been easy, and Kathy says now with remarkable candor, "If I were to say now, it's 1996 again, and I would know what it would take to get all of this done, back then I don't think I would have necessarily had the courage to take it all on. I think it was just because I kept taking a step at a time, and it led me in this direction, that I was comfortable with that."

Kathy says she met strong resistance when she tried to launch a new research model based on collaboration. "Everything you are doing is against the grain, especially with the consortium," she explained. "Everything is broken, and you are using a new model to fix it. There are so many naysayers and so much negativity when you try to do that that it's just more stressful than the other things I was doing."

Kathy also found it difficult, as she put it, to "never leave cancer." She fields calls from doctors and patients seven days a week, usually because someone isn't doing well. "So many people relapse and die around me. It's not like people remember to call and say, 'I just tried this drug that you guys brought to market and I just called to say thank you.' It's usually—and this is to be expected—'Kathy, I've relapsed, and I just don't know what to do. Can you please help me?' So that's the struggle. It takes a toll—never leaving the disease."

From fertility treatments, to fighting her cancer, to establishing and running the multiple myeloma foundation and consortium, Kathy Giusti's story is one of extraordinary perseverance over many years and through countless obstacles and disappointments. Perhaps most remarkably, she is now alive 15 years after she received a diagnosis that was tantamount to a death sentence, largely due to her own efforts toward finding a cure for the disease.

On the surface, perseverance is not a difficult trait to understand or identify in ourselves and others. It's commonly referred to as *stick-to-itiveness, determination, persistence, hardheadedness,* or just good old-fashioned *stubbornness*.[1] In one important study, perseverance is referred to as grit and explained as "working strenuously toward challenges, maintaining effort and interest over years despite failure, adversity, and plateaus in progress."[2] According to the researchers, "The gritty individual approaches achievement as a marathon; his or her advantage is stamina. Whereas disappointment or boredom signals to others that it is time to change trajectory and cut losses, the gritty individual stays the course." Perseverance is certainly not unique to our interviewees, or to any one profession or group of people. It is present, in some form or another, whenever an individual is steadfast and passionate about what he or she is doing and manages to persist through numerous difficulties toward the achievement of a long-term personal or professional goal.

What is perhaps unique to our interviewees is the context in which they persevere. Each in his or her own way is willing to buck a strong headwind to help someone else in need. Many of them could have simply walked away when the going got tough. In this regard, perseverance, the sixth choice along the path, may well be their most admirable trait and the truest measure of their character. Kathy Giusti, for example, could have abandoned her efforts to bring medical researchers together when it became clear that getting them to adopt this approach would require an intense and sustained effort on her part. Or she could have stopped taking the 7-days-a-week flood of phone calls from other multiple myeloma patients and focused exclusively on her own life-threatening challenge. But that's not the way she chose to play the cards she was dealt. She was convinced that getting researchers to work collaboratively could be life changing for patients with multiple myeloma, and so she worked hard to make that happen. And she listened to the difficulties of others and offered encouragement and solutions, even if it meant "never leaving the disease." In short, she showed the determination that enabled her to keep going even when she was emotionally and physically spent.

Perseverance allows people to persist in achieving their goals even when they meet formidable obstacles along the way. We observed three insights among our interviewees that help us understand what's at the root of their propensity for perseverance. First, they accept that frustration is inherent in the work they are striving to do, and so they are able to manage it in a productive way. Second, they are adaptable to changing circumstances when difficulties arise. Third, they remain optimistic in the face of disappointments along the way.

## Sign Up for the Frustration

Sometimes perseverance takes the form of overcoming the frustration that can arise with seeing a purpose or goal thwarted by other people or events. Consider the case of Dr. David J. Winchester, the cancer surgeon who, as we saw in Chapter 2, traveled to Russia and Latvia to perform and teach lifesaving surgery. On their first trip to Russia, David and his team brought with them dozens of boxes of donated medical equipment and supplies for the local doctors to use after the Americans had gone. The only problem was that when the team returned to Russia for the second time, they discovered that some of the equipment they had brought on the previous trip was missing, possibly sold on the black market. To say the least, it was dispiriting. David and his team had spent a great deal of time teaching the Russian doctors and nurses how to use the new equipment, which had tremendous value for patients in surgery. "The medical people still seemed very gracious and welcoming and interested, but then you kind of wonder if it was your skills and knowledge they were after or the donations you are bringing," David commented.

Perhaps one of the more easily traceable forms of frustration is feeling, or knowing, we have been bilked. David and his team gave up valuable time and considerable effort only to end up questioning whether they had been used. If we stand in the emotionality of that moment—$250,000 of equipment all gone—it's easy to understand how it could have provoked the inner skeptic in any of us to conclude: "The cards are stacked against any meaningful improvement here. It's just not worth it. We've been used. Let's pack up and go home." But that was not David's response.

This experience led David and his team members to stop, regroup, and ask a few fundamental questions: "What are we trying to do here?" "What are our goals and what are we trying to accomplish with these people?" By refocusing on their original goals of helping patients, the team was able to come to terms with the missing equipment and, perhaps more troubling, with the ulterior motives that might have been at work. "Patients are patients," David concluded, "and no question we helped some people over there, and that never changes. Their trust and their gratitude never changed, so it's just the experience of being able to go to a foreign country like that, and experience is an intriguing, amazing event."

Or think back to Susie Krabacher, the former *Playboy* centerfold turned social activist, whom we first met in the introduction to this book. Susie's work with poor women and children in Haiti has been a case study in frustration, marked by one potentially discouraging experience after another. Corruption is at the center of much that goes wrong.

In a country with shockingly high infant mortality, one of the most poignant experiences Susie told us about concerned the fate of many of the babies that she and her husband, Joe, have buried. Susie purchases a Styrofoam casket and a burial plot for the deceased infants in her care. "I'd always put a little note in the casket saying, in this world you were loved, and I would sign my name," she said. "I wanted them to know, somehow when they got to heaven they would know that this world did have somebody that loved them, somebody that held them and missed and cared about them."

But, Susie told us, it soon became apparent that the corruption that marks Haitian society was at work, even in this cemetery. "After burying so many children, I started realizing it seemed like I was burying some of the babies that died in the exact place as the old ones." Susie started investigating and found that people were digging up the Styrofoam coffins she purchased and reselling them. Sadly, she also discovered telltale bits of ragged clothing and baby skulls scattered about. Susie told us that she documented all this on film because "it is just so unbelievable that somebody would dig up a coffin, toss it aside, and sell it again to somebody else. I asked very nonchalantly what it would cost me this time if they kept the body buried. Oh, that would be an extra $75."

Equally frustrating has been the difficulty Susie has experienced trying to bring a doctor in to treat children in the abandoned infant unit of the government hospital. "I can't bring a doctor in to treat these children because I'm not willing to pay bribes. Their excuse is, well, we're a government public institution, so we can't have you bringing in your own private doctor. Okay, give me one of your doctors. Well, they can't pay anything. Well, let me hire a doctor. Well, then you have to hire one of our doctors. It just goes on and on."

Pragmatic, idealistic, but also realistic, Susie has proved to be relentlessly resilient in the face of such frustration. She draws strength and motivation from the children in her care. "I look down at these little children's faces, and they hear me arguing on their behalf, and I just see that for a moment they get that somebody is fighting for them, somebody is really fighting for them who is not going to quit." Susie commented on the corruption that she has encountered too many times in the course of her work and her stamina for dealing with it, "I don't think that I can expect fairness in the world in which I live. I think that I've got about 80 years on this planet, maybe 90, and I think I can deal with the unfairness, the injustice of corrupt people, for that amount of time."

When we are pushed to the limits of what is fair and reasonable, it can make for an uneven emotional response. But David Winchester and Susie Krabacher were not immobilized by the frustration. They each managed to navigate their way through their multilayered emotions, detaching themselves from the frustration long enough to make peace with the moment and refocus their energy on an important, humanitarian goal. They are not naïve. They know some people take advantage of others. Neither are they inclined to let that stop them. They remind themselves it's not about their frustration; it's about those they came to help.

As with all of our interviewees, David and Susie sign up for the frustrations that can accompany helping those in need. To them, signing up begins with recognizing and understanding the context of a problem. If it's a complex, long-standing problem, the potential for frustration is that much greater. Our interviewees don't grind on the incompetence of others, or the shortcomings of institutional systems, or even the sleight-of-hand canoodling that tries to take advantage of easy prey. They understand that conditions such as these allow social problems to persist. They know such work is never effortless, and nothing about it is linear. There can be false starts, setbacks, and a herky-jerky rhythm to any noticeable progress. But to them it's more than swooping in, encountering obstacles, and opting out. They calculate the frustrations as not outweighing the value of the goal or their effort. They stick with it because they believe in their reason for doing it in the first place.

## Be Adaptable

For some of our interviewees, facing down obstacles has actually strengthened their organization or effort in the long run. But turning an obstacle into an opportunity requires a certain mind-set, one of resilience, resourcefulness, and adaptability. This was the experience of Harry Leibowitz, founder of World of Children, the organization that helps children in need around the world by raising awareness and recognizing those who have made a significant difference in the lives of children.

Harry told us he came up with the idea for World of Children while he was recuperating from cancer surgery in 1996. While watching television, Harry said, he noticed that awards like the Pulitzer and Nobel prizes were given out for excellence in fields such as journalism, chemistry, and economics, but that there were no prizes for those who helped children. "If you're going to give out a prize for someone who wrote a great play, isn't it also important to give out a prize for somebody who helps children?" Harry asked. A successful business executive at the time, Harry worked for 2 years on a plan for what would become the World of Children. In 1998, the organization gave out its first award. Since then, World of Children has awarded cash grants to 90 humanitarians working in more than 51 countries worldwide.

When we asked Harry what the biggest obstacle was that he encountered in leading World of Children, his answer was immediate and emphatic. "We were getting $250,000 a year from two corporate donors, and in the same year, they both pulled out. So $500,000 of our $610,000 budget was gone that year. We made it but we had to struggle." Harry said he was extremely dejected at the time, but his wife galvanized his energy and optimism by reminding him of a favorite adage of his former boss and mentor Brian Lees: "There are no problems, just opportunities."

In the end, Harry said, the loss of the two large donations helped World of Children build a more sustainable model of funding. "We changed our operation," Harry told us. "We started talking to people we knew and said we have to raise this money ourselves. The first thing was one of our board members came forward and said, I'm going to put up $50,000 as a challenge grant, so that turned into $100,000." Harry said that they just "begged and borrowed," even cut the amount of the awards they gave out to $50,000, but they did make it through the year. "Now, we're going to be able to go back to $100,000 because we have a better template and a better organization. In an odd sort of way, using Brian's lesson, it was a crisis that turned into an opportunity that has made us bigger, stronger, and better."

Sometimes things don't go as planned. Furthermore, as Harry experienced, sometimes it can all come unraveled at once. As he watched nearly all of the funding for World of Children evaporate before his eyes, Harry was faced with two choices. He could say it was a great idea that just wasn't sustainable and then give up, or he could adapt to his new circumstance. Harry adapted. He viewed his new environment not as a problem, but as an "opportunity" to rethink, redesign, and reimagine the possibilities. After all, Harry didn't see the concept of World of Children as a passing interest. He saw it as a lifelong obligation within his jurisdiction as a responsible human being.

Our interviewees know nothing is formulaic. They know their planned effort may or may not be an uncomplicated experience. They don't disadvantage themselves with inflexibility. When presented with an unexpected thorny circumstance, adjustments are creatively invented. In their own way, they each adroitly improvise as needed and move forward smartly and swiftly between challenges. They know that to step forward, sometimes we first need to step outside of our own assumptions and adapt. They also know, as we learn from Harry, adapting can make a lost opportunity reappear.

## Remain Optimistic

Stories abound among our interviewees of surmounting formidable obstacles on the way to reaching their goals. Often the obstacle is in the form of a direct threat to one's own optimism. Central to maintaining one's optimism is not losing the positive attitude we discussed in the previous chapter.

For more than 25 years, Sherri Kirkpatrick has brought mother-child health care education to women in some of the poorest countries of the world, including Haiti, the Democratic Republic of Congo, and Malawi. But she also has experienced the disappointment of establishing programs that help people in need and then being kept out of a country for long periods because of political unrest.

"I really had to come to grips with it because my very first experience, in Haiti, it wasn't long before that whole project was gone because of the political situation there. The different countries that I have gone into, the Congo, there were long periods of time when I couldn't get in there." Sherri told us she has come to terms with such impromptu and disruptive changes by remembering that "if you give somebody education, nobody can take it away. You may not be able to get supplies to them, but you can't take the education away, and you can't take the self-esteem away that they now feel."

She added, reflecting a shorter-term perspective that may be more realistic in the unstable countries in which she works, "My philosophy is, you really can't dwell on the future, you only have today. And if you can help somebody's life today, or make life easier for them, then it's worth it. You'd like to think, we all do, that everything that we're doing is going to grow and be a permanent value, but that's not true with all the projects that I've worked with, other than the fact that once you've given a mother knowledge, she for sure is going to pass that knowledge along to her children."

Sherri has lived in extremely harsh conditions in some of the countries in which she works. One particularly uncomfortable experience involved taking an icy shower in Malawi when she was suffering from a severe sinus infection. "There is no heat in the homes, and usually you have to go outside to take a shower," she explained. "They did have water piped into this little house where we were staying, but it was cold, frigid cold. I remember looking at the spout and thinking, I'm going to put my head under that cold water, and thinking I am here by choice. I can't believe I'm here by choice."

But, Sherri says, it's ultimately the health care workers she trains who inspire her to keep going. "These are people—mostly women—who get up at 4:30 and 5:00 a.m. in the dark, walk to the river to get the water for the day, stumble back in the dark to bring it to their families, find the wood to heat their fires, pound the grain because most of them don't have flour mills, and almost all of this is with a baby on their back. This is their life. In addition to that, they volunteer to be a health worker. That usually means walking a long distance to another village where they are even less well off than the volunteer village would be. Weighing the babies and teaching them about how to treat leg ulcers and doing incredible things for no pay, but feeling good about it and doing it year after year. That's where you really get your inspiration, when you see how eagerly people embrace the little bit of knowledge you give them." These aid workers have their own considerable obstacles to overcome, but the rewards that come with helping mothers and children lead healthier lives inspire them to persevere, just as the goals of our interviewees have motivated them in the face of adversity.

If optimism is encouraged by a chance to make a difference, then pessimism is abetted by an inability to get at a problem and at least try. Imagine the threat to optimism if one is kept from continuing toward a goal. But Sherri remains optimistic knowing she has started efforts that found the right people, those who understand the value of mother-child health care and who will continue the momentum. With this optimism and her globetrotting adaptability, Sherri continues to work through our multicultural world of customs, practices, priorities, and problems. She may not know whether she or her efforts will be accepted or tolerated, or for how long, but she perseveres and her optimism remains intact.

No one wants to be drawn into an orbit that wastes their time or violates their expectations. All of our interviewees know their initial high hopes may get lowered along the way, but they remain positive about their ability to matter. The relentless phone calls from individuals asking for help and understanding while trying to cope with one's own cancer as well as trying to create a different model for cancer research, the unexplained disappearance of surgical equipment, the perversity of infant grave robbing, the evaporation of funding, and the oppressive tension of being kept from continuing to help can all throw optimism into a free fall. But none of these wearing disruptions to their efforts erodes our interviewees' optimism. They try, they are tripped up, they trust their goal, and they try again.

The irony, of course, is the simplicity of helping others can become disappointingly complicated. As we learned from our interviewees, if the goal is worth pursuing, perseverance is probably required. It's reasonable to expect some degree of frustration, it's important to be adaptable to changing circumstances, and it's essential to remain optimistic in the face of disappointment. All of our interviewees, like Kathy Giusti, played the cards they were dealt.

But the stories of our interviewees are more than individual narratives of perseverance. Combined, they show us more than the chore of staying with it. They show us the only way to remedy the ills of humanity is not to be stymied by the obstacles that present themselves on the way to a solution. Our interviewees seem to know if we all backpedal when discouraged, then nothing is possible. Without trying to be, through their perseverance, they are role models for taking charge of a better society. They teach us not to be discouraged into a lesser world.

Calvin Coolidge famously said about persistence, but he could have easily used the word perseverance: "Nothing in the world can take the place of persistence. . . . The slogan, 'press on,' has solved and always will solve the problems of the human race."

Those who persevere are more likely to attract and inspire others to get involved as well. This is the seventh choice we identified, and it is explored in the next chapter, "Leading the Way."

## Do You Persevere When the Going Gets Tough?

1. Kathy Giusti persevered through seemingly endless obstacles, including a disease that posed a constant threat to her life. What qualities and abilities as a person and leader does Kathy exhibit that help explain how she was able to keep going and meet the goals she had set for herself?

2. Dr. David J. Winchester and his team faced understandable frustration when the medical supplies they had brought to Russia

from the United States suddenly disappeared. How was the team able to deal with their frustration? Why is signing up for the frustration such an important element of perseverance? Have you dealt with similar frustration during a volunteer experience? How were you able to handle it?

3. Sometimes charting a different course in the face of changing circumstances, as Harry Leibowitz of World of Children did, is the only way to move forward. Why is being adaptable so important if one is to persevere? Can you think of an experience in your own life when you had to adapt to new circumstances in order to succeed? Do you believe that adaptability is a key element in effective leadership? Why?

4. American president Calvin Coolidge said, "Nothing in the world can take the place of persistence." He further noted, "Talent will not; nothing is more common than unsuccessful men with talent. Genius will not; unrewarded genius is almost a proverb. Education will not; the world is full of educated derelicts. Persistence and Determination alone are omnipotent." What are your thoughts on Coolidge's perspective?

5. Can the importance of perseverance be overstated? Are there ever times when wisdom and experience dictate that a helping effort be abandoned? Have you ever had this experience? How would an effective leader handle this scenario?

# 7

# Leading the Way

## *Shame Hung Over the Sanctuary*

I n our interview with Jennifer Atler, at the time executive director of the Colorado-based nonprofit organization Invest in Kids, we asked her if she approached her goals with a particular "frame of mind" and if she had any knowledge or understanding of where that frame of mind came from. Her answer was unequivocal. "Absolutely, I can tell you the exact moment that I decided that this is what I wanted to do." And Jennifer told us the deeply disturbing story that we referred to in Chapter 1.

"My mom is a survivor of child sexual abuse and a former Miss America," Jennifer began, explaining that her mother, Marilyn Van Derbur, whose abuser was her own father, had done a lot of national speaking and was very well known, but that no one knew about her past.

"A newspaper reporter found out about it and basically took it public. We woke up one morning, and it was on the front page of the paper. And it stayed on the front page for a week." Jennifer told us that after the news broke, her mother turned off the phones, shut the blinds, and went into hiding for a couple of days.

"She was sure that no one would ever want to speak to her again, and all of those horrible things that survivors, or victims, feel,"

Jennifer said. "But very soon her sister came forward and substantiated what had happened."

Jennifer's parents were at a local high school running around the track when a woman approached her mother and said, "I'm so glad your sister came forward because now people will have to believe you."

Her mother asked the woman what she meant, and the woman replied, "I was listening to the radio this morning, and they said that your father is dead and you, of course, could accuse him of this, and he has no way to speak up for himself. They said now people are going to have to believe you because your sister came forward too."

The woman's words had a profound effect on Jennifer's mother, who understood that if "they" would not believe a 53-year-old woman, then "they" were not likely to believe a child who was talking about sexual abuse.

At that point, Jennifer told us, her mother took the courageous step of arranging a meeting at a local church. The meeting wasn't publicized, but word of the gathering spread quickly throughout the community. Jennifer, who was home from college that weekend, attended this meeting and remembers clearly what happened. "There were 1,100 people who showed up at that meeting. I walked in, and my favorite elementary school teacher was there, and my best friend's mother was there, and no one was speaking. Just shame hung over that sanctuary, like you couldn't even imagine the feeling in that room."

That night changed Jennifer's life. "That was it," she said. "I knew from then on that I wanted to work for kids, women too, but mostly children so that, hopefully, 20 to 30 years from now there wouldn't need to be 1,100 people in that room." She added, "That was when I really decided that was the path that I wanted to take."

## Completing the Path

Jennifer Atler both embodies and illustrates the path our 31 remarkable interviewees have followed and that we have described in the previous chapters. In this chapter, we explore how Jennifer and our other interviewees came to lead others by creating and building a collective energy and enthusiasm for achieving a goal—the seventh and last choice along the path. But first, let us remind you of the preceding choices we observed as they show up in Jennifer's story.

Jennifer clearly illustrates the essential feature of the first choice we identified, making a connection and then leveraging that connection and other life experiences into helping others. Her world changed that weekend she was home from college. The news that her mother had been sexually exploited by, of all people, Jennifer's grandfather; the word-of-mouth meeting that resulted in more than 1,000 attendees, some of whom she knew while growing up but that she was now experiencing in a different and very emotionally intense climate; her return to school and her need for some time alone to examine the new meanings coursing through her life were a few of the many life experiences confronting Jennifer. For some of our interviewees, these life experiences came as the proverbial bolt of lightning. For others, they came as a gradual accumulation of awareness.

These new life experiences allowed Jennifer to empathize, to feel in some perhaps small but nevertheless significant way, what another person was feeling. And that feeling was mentally, physically, emotionally, and spiritually painful. To connect with that pain, to touch it, and to feel it at some level is to experience empathy.

This connection we have described takes on an additional dimension in our interviewees when they also experience a strong sense of unfairness. Jennifer's story also illustrates this second choice. Few circumstances cry out for empathy more strongly than the sexual exploitation of a child by a powerful adult in a position of trust. For the sexually exploited child, the injustice of not being believed intensifies the psychological torment. Jennifer, like all our interviewees, recognizes and acknowledges the lack of justice, the absence of fundamental fairness, in the circumstances with which some other human beings must cope. When coupled with a connection based on empathy, that sense of unfairness becomes a powerful motivator to take action.

The third choice our interviewees made on the inner path is the one we call believing we can matter. As we discussed earlier, most of us find it relatively easy to make this choice—in the opposite direction. After all, what can we really do? Even in the presence of the greatest pain and the most intense injustice, what can one person do? The easiest choice, of course, the one that requires almost no effort, is to do nothing. We can easily talk ourselves into this alternative, and even convince ourselves that to do nothing is the most reasonable, rational, and intelligent choice.

For Jennifer, the choice to continue her life as it was would have been easy. After that weekend at home, she went back to school. She was a sophomore at Duke University at the time. She described herself as a "fast-track economics major." She said she was headed for "somewhere in the business world." As she explained, "My dad, before I could even talk, was talking business deals with me. That's his passion, so I always thought I'd follow in his footsteps and do something around the business world."

But she decided to go to law school instead. And this decision created a new focus for her emotional and spiritual energies. She wanted to help mothers and children in need, particularly children, and a law degree would allow her to do that. A new set of priorities emerged around that decision. New interests reinforced that decision. New activities provided fuel for the time and energy that defined that decision. In fact, if we believe the collective voices of the 31 people in this study, there can be little doubt that this decision gave Jennifer and her life a new meaning and purpose. She had come to believe she had what it took to make a meaningful difference in the lives of mothers and children in need.

We have concluded from our research that the critical quality of the new path and where it ultimately leads is determined by the extent to which our interviewees, including Jennifer, remained open to opportunities, the fourth choice. As you recall, when Jennifer was a new law school graduate in a high-powered firm, she nevertheless let her interests in the rights of children be known. Soon, an opportunity to act in the direction of the needs of children presented itself. Jennifer was invited by a senior member of her firm to attend meetings of a fledgling organization called Invest in Kids.

She was immediately intrigued by the passion and commitment of the founders of the group, community leaders who were concerned about the disparities in achievement between higher and lower income students in Colorado, as well as the increasing number of crimes committed by young people from poorer families. As we saw,

Jennifer began to take small steps to get involved in this new organization, the fifth choice along the path.

Before long, she was taking advantage of every opportunity to be of help to this group of people who had the audacity to believe they could make a difference in the lives of children. It's worth noting that at any point, Jennifer could have made a choice that would have taken her off the path, uninvolved in doing anything about the problems that beset low-income children in Colorado. But through funding difficulties, legislative challenges, and other obstacles, Jennifer consistently made the sixth choice and persevered.

Soon Jennifer was out in communities leading others. She helped groups of citizens evaluate social programs, write proposals, obtain funding, and do whatever needed to be done for the children in their communities. In a relatively short time, and with the full support of the partners in her firm, Jennifer left her law firm and became executive director of Invest in Kids within the first year.

Jennifer is quite typical of our interviewees. Her story moves from an inner world to an outward focus. Leading oneself before leading others. She is the essence of what is meant by the oft-given advice from teachers and scholars of leadership to "follow your passion."

The commitment of our interviewees has created energy in others that has led to broader efforts that have affected, in concrete ways, millions of children and adults all over the world. This is *transformational* leadership at its best, what the eminent scholar James MacGregor Burns describes as leadership with a moral dimension that "raises the level of human conduct and ethical aspiration of both leader and led." Burns further explains that transformational leadership is "dynamic leadership in the sense that the leaders throw themselves into a relationship with followers who will feel 'elevated' by it and often become more active themselves, thereby creating new cadres of leaders."[1]

Some of our interviewees have created rather large organizations and sizeable infrastructures for managing the efforts of people who have been permanently changed by the passions of these extraordinary individuals. Our interviewees have become leaders. But we don't think any of them intentionally started out to become leaders. Rather, leadership grew naturally as their focus on the goal of improving the lives of others shaped the nature of the relationship between themselves and others.

## Creating Contagion

Attitudes are very contagious. Emotional and behavioral contagion is a well-established phenomenon. Folk wisdom reminds us in hundreds of different ways that "Attitudes are contagious—is yours worth catching?" "Laugh and the world laughs with you." "Anger begets anger." In addition, social scientists from four different disciplines—communication, psychology, sociology, and political science—have all made a similar discovery: Behavior is contagious between people in relationships.[2]

Jennifer Atler's attitude, and the resulting energy and enthusiasm, has transferred to the people who work at Invest in Kids. She described the staff as "can-do, positive, totally mission driven, and passionate." Jennifer observed, "I think the magic has definitely carried from our founders to our leadership and down to our staff."

When they are out talking with others about the early childhood programs they would like to help communities adopt, that commitment transfers to the members of the citizen groups that work together to bring the early childhood programs into their communities. When those citizen groups are successful in bringing one of the early childhood programs into their communities, the commitment of the citizen group members transfers to the people managing the program and from the managers of the programs to the nurses and teachers delivering the programs to children and families. Recent research has described Invest in Kids' site development process as a "transfer of commitment" model and has documented the fact that the early attitudes of the process leaders are still affecting the success of the programs 4 to 5 years after the original community meetings have been completed.[3]

This emotional and behavioral contagion, or transfer of commitment, originating from a dedicated leader, is precisely why it is possible for Craig Kielburger to stand up in front of his seventh grade class, tell a story, ask for help from his classmates, and 16 years later find himself leading a worldwide organization with a million young people involved in its programs.

One of our other interviewees talked about how she caught Craig Kielburger's attitude. Cheryl Perera told it this way. "It was the last few days of my tenth grade civics class and we had just finished our final exam. Our teacher gave us a list of nonprofit organizations, and we were supposed to pick one and do research on it. Given that the exam was over, I wasn't too thrilled about doing more work, so I went to the teacher and I complained." While Cheryl was complaining, the rest of the students had taken all of the organizations, and the last one on the list was one called Free The Children.

"So I ended up dragging myself to the library, and I took out the book that Craig Kielburger had written. I was not expecting anything at all; I was just going to read this book for the purpose of doing this project, and I wanted to get an A and I'd be content. As I was reading it, it was starting to affect me. And I got to the point where Craig talks about his time in Thailand in Pat Pong, the red light district where child prostitution is rampant."

While she was alone with the book, Cheryl's life changed. "I was so shocked by what I read. I thought about my life, and even though we did grow up in the beginning in poverty, my parents gave me everything they could. I had an education, I was happy. I had a childhood. These kids didn't. The difference in my life and their life was so astounding that I knew I had to take action."

Fast forward several months. Still in high school, Cheryl has arranged through her principal to make a study abroad trip to Sri Lanka for the purpose of investigating child exploitation practices. She has learned that some countries have child sex tourism industries, where hotels offer perpetrators special deals, and child sex tours are arranged.

Soon, Cheryl was working in an undercover sting operation. Once the contact had been made online, the perpetrator expressed his interest and wanted to meet the child to see what he or she looked like. "They had groomed this relationship for a while and I came in at the right time to play the role of the girl," Cheryl explained. "We met him in broad daylight, in an outdoor restaurant. I had been working with the police. I basically took the file home and learned everything.

I had to know exactly what the story was. If he asked me any questions, I had to be able to come up with something right away."

As it turned out, Cheryl played her part to perfection. The predator was entirely convinced that she was an underage prostitute and made lurid and detailed propositions to her, all of which were recorded by Cheryl on a spy camera attached to her purse. After observing this conversation as plainclothes customers, the police swooped in to arrest the offender.

Cheryl's story is a dramatic example of where emotional contagion can lead. In Cheryl's case, it started in a quiet library where she was immersed in a book. A year and a half later, it was at full speed halfway around the world as she sat in an outdoor restaurant alone with a child sex offender. One of the most interesting things about this emotional contagion is that even the people who have it typically do not know where it will lead. They are, quite simply, following their passion.

An interesting case that further illustrates the contagious quality of this commitment is Peter Samuelson. As he told us, "My career as a film producer consists almost entirely of trying to persuade people to do things that they don't really want to do. Whereas, when I have my prosocial hat on, generally speaking, two out of three people that I ask for help say sure, let me see if I can help you."

Starlight, the foundation Peter created to help seriously ill children, has thousands of volunteers. Peter said, "Sometimes I sneak up to the office late on a Sunday night and there are 40 people sitting in there doing things. Why are they there? Well, because they care. They care about the life force; they care about lifting up their planet and making a difference."

Peter described one of his early experiences in Hollywood encountering the power of emotional contagion: "In 1990 I realized that we had branched out of wish granting considerably and one of the things that we had done is that we had several thousand audiovisual installations in children's hospitals, and we were showing every variety of children's software, videotapes, DVDs and the rest of it, but nothing was particularly helpful for the children. Just sort of general kids distracted entertainment."

Fortunately, Peter could approach a filmmaker who knew a thing or two about how to appeal to a young audience. He arranged a first meeting with director Steven Spielberg, during which he described his organization's huge physical audiovisual distribution network serving the world of pediatric patients. He presented some thoughts about making software programming for children who are seriously ill. Peter told us, "He got very interested in that. It was supposed to be a 15-minute meeting, and I came out almost 3 hours later."

Toward the end of the meeting, Spielberg asked what Peter wanted him to do. "I said, 'Well, you be the chairman and we will call it Starbright because that's the second word of the children's rhyme, and Starbright will put a board together, and we'll raise some money and get on it and do this.' He said, 'Okay, I should probably make a gift, shouldn't I, because how can I be the chairman if I don't lead from the front.' I said, 'That would be great.' He said, 'How much do you think I should give?' I said, 'That's entirely up to you, Steven.' He said, 'No, just give me a number.'

"I have no idea what possessed me, but I had an out-of-body experience where I saw my mouth say to Steven, 'two million, two-and-a-half million dollars.' And he said, 'Okay, that will be fine.' I remember I came out and hid behind a tree and called my wife and said that I think I just had a hallucination."

Peter's story, in which he surprised even himself with the magnitude of his request to Spielberg, illustrates something else we discovered among most, if not all, of our interviewees: An increased level of courage, or nerve, comes with commitment to a worthwhile goal.

Time after time, as we listen to these extraordinary people sharing moments of their life's stories, we are drawn invariably to some fundamental conclusions about leadership. Leadership originates from inside an individual. It's an outward expression of an internal state. It is expressed in action that is directed toward some end, some vision, goal, value, or cause. To the extent that the individual is acting out of a connection with others that is strengthened or deepened by the individual's life experiences and exhibits a commitment that others recognize, to some degree, in themselves, then those others are more likely to be influenced by the act.

A collective energy and enthusiasm is created by commitment. This energy can be seen in the contrast between active versus passive behavior, positive versus negative attitude, optimism versus cynicism, hope versus despair, and all those contrasts that cause us to attribute credibility to another and have greater confidence in the direction offered. The energy and enthusiasm that accompany one person's commitment can be, and often are, transferred from one person to another. That this transfer of commitment ultimately realizes the vision or accomplishes the goal is self-evident.

Listen to Larry Bradley describe his interaction with a struggling soldier in his unit, and you will see how powerful this transfer of commitment, energy, and vision by a dedicated leader can be. "One of my soldiers was having a hard time over in Iraq, a real hard time emotionally. We were hit a few times by roadside bombs, and he didn't want to go out anymore. He said, 'I can't do this,' and we had about 2 months left."

So, Larry began to talk to the soldier about goals. "'When you got here, what was your goal?' He said it was to get home alive. I said, 'Okay, but what were your other goals?' He said it was to do the best he could. I said, 'Okay, if you were to sit on this base now for 2 months, and you go home, you may still go home alive, mortar rounds come in all the time, you still might get killed, but there is a good chance you will get home alive. But will you sit at home and say that I did the best I could, or I did everything I could do over there?' I tried to lay out the different goals that he didn't even know he had. I put that out in front of him, and he said, 'You're right.'"

After Larry talked with the soldier about his goals, the man became reinvigorated. "He could go home and look himself in the mirror." The soldier became Larry's driver and went out on every mission, always fully prepared. Larry assured the soldier, "I'm sure you'll be okay out there with me because my goal is to get home alive too." In the end, the soldier completed his tour of duty and returned home safely.

Larry told us with some pride that even though the soldier lives in New Hampshire, he traveled several times to New Orleans to help rebuild after Hurricane Katrina struck. Larry still stays in touch with the man. "He told me, 'You know what, when we sat down and we laid out what I wanted, I wasn't going to let anything make me complacent about that.' He was going to get to those goals."

In this chapter, we saw repeatedly the powerful difference one person's leadership can make. This difference is captured in the words of Kathy Giusti, of the Multiple Myeloma Research Foundation, who observed, "If someone has the courage to step ahead and lead, it is amazing how many people will work with you to make sure you get the job done." Now, in the following chapter, we turn our attention to the collective impact the efforts of our 31 interviewees have had on our global society.

## Are You Ready to Lead?

1. Jennifer Atler's story illustrates how important it is to follow your passion. She connected with an issue on a deeply personal level and began by leading herself before she progressed to leading others. Why do you think Jennifer became so effective in her role at Invest in Kids? What can you learn from her experience? What do we mean by leading oneself first?

2. It is now well accepted that attitudes are contagious. Have you had an experience as a leader when your attitude was "caught" by others? Are you aware of a time when you "caught" the attitude of a leader?

3. Major Larry Bradley has shown his leadership skills not only in action in Iraq but also in quiet moments talking with a troubled soldier. What does that tell you about good leadership? What lessons can be learned by the way Larry handled the challenge of convincing a soldier who had been traumatized on the field to return to his mission?

4. Our interviewees represent a wide range of ages and cultures. Do you think there are generational differences in leadership? Are there cultural differences?

5. In this book, we focus heavily on the personal connections between people. However, in the 21st century, we recognize that technology, including social networking media, has had a wide impact on raising awareness of, and even solving, societal problems. Can you think of ways in which you could use social media and other technologies to become a more effective humanitarian leader?

6. In this chapter, the path of choices is completed, using Jennifer Atler's story as an illustration. If you are involved in a helping effort, where would you place yourself now on the path? Can you trace the path that we outline in this book in your own life?

7. James MacGregor Burns describes transformational leadership as a relationship of mutual elevation that converts followers into leaders.[4] What does Burns mean by this? When you think about Jennifer Atler's story in particular, how does her experience illustrate this relationship between leaders and followers? Have you ever known someone you would consider to be a transformational leader? Why would you characterize this leader in this way?

# 8

# A Positive Force

*The Accumulation of Good*

There is good in the world. There is bad in the world. The tension between these two forces is constant. The goal of any society is to create enough positive force to diminish the negative. Sometimes this is accomplished by government, sometimes by private citizens. We don't have to stretch our imaginations very far to know what happens when the negatives outweigh the positives. There is enough archival evidence. As all of history has shown, some people suffer, usually those with less say over their lives and grimmer prospects for life going well.

The second law of thermodynamics teaches us that anything left unattended will tend toward decay. From fitness to flossing to friendships, everything requires constant attention. While the ills of the world may never be eliminated, there must be a constant positive force pushing back against the negative. It is the tension between two archetypes: development versus decay. Our 31 interviewees understand this ongoing tension. They also understand the high metabolism of social decay. They know that if social problems are left unattended, bad will prevail.

So, a teacher in India brings education to more than 4,000 impoverished children in slums and at railway platforms, and also provides social services for their families. A 6-year-old boy spends his next 10 years helping to build more than 630 wells and other water projects in countries where disease and even geographic skirmishes revolve around access to drinkable water and farmable land. A pediatrician dedicates his life to reducing disease and premature death and promoting healthy living in Africa and the United States, resulting in a better life for more than 1.5 million people. A nurse helps found an organization that has performed more than 160,000 surgeries to correct facial deformities. A former journalist in Taiwan creates programs and shelters that have protected more than 150,000 children from sexual exploitation or abuse. A woman spearheads an organization that feeds more than 5,000 women and children a day in Haiti and also runs two orphanages. Would the world go on without them? For some, yes; for others, no.

All you have to do is run your eyes down the right side of Figure 8.1[1] to see that all 10 of the loosely grouped categories of problems addressed by our interviewees defy human decency. Some of the problems we have created ourselves. Others have been created by circumstance. Many are rooted in a lack of fundamental respect for human potential.

The problems our interviewees address are so large any effort seems small by comparison, and any perceptible progress agonizingly gradual. Consider just one example, the sexual exploitation of children. Harry Leibowitz, founder of World of Children, offers a thoughtful analysis in an unpublished white paper he has prepared. As he discovered in the course of his research, sexual exploitation of young people has existed throughout history. In some societies— Thailand is just one example—it has been abetted by the absence of basic laws that would make it a punishable offense.

In fact, the magnitude and constancy of the problem is a history lesson in ambivalence. It's hard to believe anyone cares. Few people sprint toward such problems. The reality is most of us spend our lives distancing ourselves from them. But among our interviewees, Hui-jung Chi, Craig Kielburger, Sanphasit Koompraphant, and Cheryl Perera all address the problem in various countries around the world. They are part of a positive force for children. They push back.

Ronald Heifetz, a psychiatrist and senior lecturer at the Harvard Kennedy School of Government, sheds important light on just why

**Figure 8.1**  Positive and Negative Forces in Our Global Society

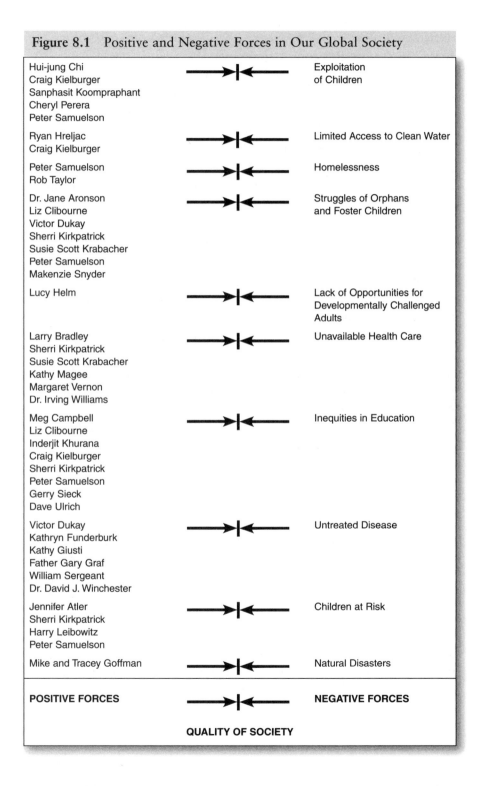

these kinds of societal problems are so extraordinarily difficult to solve.[2] In the progression of complexity, he argues, problems such as poverty, ethnic strife, and failing schools are the most intractable because they have neither clear-cut definitions nor known solutions. As a result, Heifetz explains, situations like these require a different kind of leadership, one that challenges people to "learn new ways," which may involve changing fundamental attitudes, behavior, or values. We saw the resistance a leader can face in trying to bring about such seismic shifts in thinking in the story of Sanphasit Koompraphant, who worked tirelessly for years to enact the most basic laws to protect children from abuse and exploitation in his native Thailand.

Leadership, as Heifetz defines it, isn't the province of the few in positions of authority, but as we have argued throughout this book, the domain of any citizen with the desire to make a positive difference in society. And so, in a world that always seems in peril and somehow in decline, our interviewees have been part of the positive force that has kept our global society from giving in to negative influences and, in the words of the second law of thermodynamics, decay. Each of their efforts is tantamount to a miracle in slow motion. Together their positive impact has been enormous. And they are only 31 people. But they are 31 people who are practitioners of good.

What's more, the accumulation of good encourages a climate that promotes hope over despair. Good work encourages more good work. Our interviewees traffic in hope and transfer optimism to those who watch. With the combined efforts of our interviewees, good weighs on the balance scale of society, a little more hope prevails, and our global community is, and feels, a little more fair.

We selected all of our interviewees because of what they have done, and many because of the differences they have made. But if, in our final analysis, we turn inward again, what else might we learn from our interviewees? How do they feel about the ways they have spent their time and energies? Are the problems they have tackled, indeed, overwhelming? For those of us who talked ourselves out of acting on those leadership opportunities that did present themselves, is there any vindication? These are the kinds of questions we explored at the end of each interview. Our observations are offered in the next and final chapter.

## Can Good in the World Outweigh the Bad?

1. As you consider Figure 8.1, do you believe that 31 people can have a positive impact on the world's problems? How would you assess the cumulative impact the people in this book have had? Does this help clarify your thinking on the difference one person can make?

2. Are there some problems in the world that are solvable and others that are so intractable that no amount of trying seems to make a difference? Should this stop you from trying?

3. If you think back to Chapter 2, "A Sense of Fairness," what attitudes, behaviors, and values would have to change in order to begin to solve the problem of child sexual exploitation?

4. How does good work encourage not only more good work but also an optimism that change can occur and the future can be different? What examples from history, current events, or your own experience might illustrate this point?

# 9

# A Larger Life

## *No Gravestone Has a Job Title or Salary on It*

The humanitarian leaders profiled in this book allowed us brief glimpses into their journeys of helping those in need. Their journeys are incredibly varied, yet our interviewees described them in strikingly similar ways. What's more, many of the paths they followed on the way to helping others were difficult, littered with obstacles that would cause less hardy souls to back away or quit. So it seems reasonable to wonder at this point whether their journeys have brought our interviewees to a good place. The answer we found is consistently yes. Whatever it might be called, happiness, contentment, or more recently, subjective well-being, we have found that our interviewees like where their life journeys have led them.[1]

If we return to their own words, we find our interviewees characterize their journeys in slightly different ways. Victor Dukay, you may recall, lost both parents and his sister to violence as a child and later built an orphanage in Tanzania. He said, "The Africa work has had a huge impact on me. It has helped me realize how lucky I am, how blessed I am, how fortunate I am. I've had an opportunity to use gifts I have to help others, so that they won't necessarily be in the same situation that I'm in. And, strangely enough, to give me purpose. To allow me to get out of bed, to not be depressed, to do something with my life."

Ryan Hreljac, who has helped build wells on three continents where water is scarce, noted that his work helping others has been "a two-way street." Still in his teens, he has traveled extensively and given scores of speeches. "I've gotten to do things that I would never have been able to do because of this. It's been great."

And Lucy Helm, the codirector of a camp for developmentally challenged adults, said, "The thing that intrigues me about the camp experience is how touched and changed you can be by becoming part of someone else's different experience."

Margaret Vernon, the Peace Corps volunteer, seems to have attained a highly valued clarity about life's priorities. "Being here I've come to realize how important family and health are. Life is hard; people work long hours in 110 degree heat, and hard physical labor is a fact of life. But those things become less punishing when you have your family and health."

Larry Bradley characterized his 10 months in Iraq as a "life-changing experience, both spiritually and emotionally." A Catholic, he had always gone to church on Sunday, but he told us, "I learned how to pray. I've slowed down to be more appreciative of what I've been given and what we have on earth, in the United States especially. I don't know how to describe it, but I'm more reflective now. I never really read the Bible until I went to Iraq. Everyone said to bring books, and I said I am bringing one book with me everywhere I go."

For many of our interviewees, life has taken on qualities of discovery, intrigue, even adventure. One of the many e-mails that Liz Clibourne sent to her family and friends during one of her working stints in Africa contained the following passage, punctuated by the Swahili she has learned there:

> I've been biking into Kyela every day, that's about 20 kilometers, and I haven't felt this good in a long time. But *matako yanauma*. My butt hurts. It's these cheap bicycle seats combined with the bumpy roads. Ivo, the guy I rent my bike from, has a replacement, and I'm getting it put on when I return to Ngonga. *Asante mungu*. [Thank you, God.] When I first got to the village, I rode slowly and carefully, because the road is crazy. Lately, though, I've been taking the curves and dips like the rest of these

yahoos and making pretty good time. It's too fun, the wind in my hair and all that. The bugs in my teeth are an annoyance, and I really hate it when they fly up my nose. I had a basket put on the front and I put my Discman and the portable speakers inside. I like classic rock best, and I ride at the speed of the music, singing and swerving and spitting bugs. This is the best job ever.

As we said before, these "arrivals" at new points in their journeys can be described in many different ways. But not one of our interviewees expressed disappointment with the life choices they have made. *Time* magazine essayist Nancy Gibbs summarized recent research on happiness, which includes such findings as "happiness correlates much more closely with our causes and connectedness than with our net worth." Gibbs further noted that while charitable giving declined in 2008 for the first time in two decades, "about a million more people volunteered their time to a cause." These findings led her to wonder: "Is it a coincidence that eight of the 10 happiest states in the country also rank in the top 10 for volunteering?"[2]

We have observed as well that our interviewees are not only happy with their own lives, they are also spreaders of happiness to others. Some of our interviews were conducted in person, others by telephone. In many cases, we spent time with our interviewees beyond the interview itself. We noticed that these interviewees were in social networks that impressed us as upbeat, positive, or happy. Recently, the landmark Framingham Heart Study, which has followed thousands of people over decades, reported that happiness clusters in groups, that it spreads across a wide range of social relationships, and that "clusters of happiness result from the spread of happiness and not just a tendency for people to associate with similar individuals."[3] We believe our interviewees create and spread positive emotional energy that contributes to and sustains happiness in their social networks, and they do this largely by virtue of the qualities we have described in this book.

What then accounts for the consistency in the satisfaction our interviewees have expressed, and why do they all seem to have arrived at a good point in their life journeys? We offer the following observations.

## Making a Difference Makes a Difference

The important point here is not that our interviewees made a difference. We selected them because they devoted a significant portion of their lives to helping others, and we now know that they have made a positive difference in the lives of a great many people. The important point here is that making a difference has had a profound effect on the quality of the lives of our interviewees as well. Their lives have been enriched.[4] Let us give you a few examples.

Cheryl Perera told us about "a particularly powerful moment" she experienced in the Philippines when she visited the gravesite of a young street child who had died in 1986 and whose story was publicized around the world. "Her name was Rosario Baluyot. A tourist came and picked up Rosario and another street boy, and brought them to his hotel. He physically and sexually abused Rosario." Cheryl paused before adding, "She was found on the street, and she later died of an infection. She was 12 years old."

Cheryl was talking about the difficult, emotionally draining aspect of her work. She continued, "So that's an example of what happens. How horrible this issue is. People come up with the most ridiculous things and say, in these countries children are more sexual. But in the end, this is what happens. It was so powerful for me to stand there. This is the face of the issue." Horrible though they may be, these kinds of experiences give Cheryl Perera's life meaning and purpose. They remind her of the difference she can make, and is making, in the lives of others.[5]

Reminders come in different forms. Sherri Kirkpatrick told us about a couple she met in the Congo. "His name was Nicodemus and her name was Mama Regina. Their daughter had been one of many that had suffered from leg ulcers for years. They had been able to get just enough money together to get one treatment of antibiotics every couple of years, which ended up being the worst thing they could have done, because it made the organisms resistant.

"When I came in trying to treat leg ulcers we could help her some, but we never got it totally cured," Sherri continued. "So with that in mind, knowing that their daughter did not get a complete cure of the leg ulcers like many people did, they walked probably about 6 miles with a little goat on their shoulders as a present to me, to thank me for even trying to help their daughter, and for making it better than it had been for her.

"For this couple, a goat is a huge gift," Sherri explained. "It would be like us giving somebody a car. A lot of times these people even go into debt or borrow to give a gift that they think is appropriate. It has impacted my life in a large way, thinking, you can't just take life for granted."

Dave Ulrich, the University of Michigan business professor and consultant who took a 3-year sabbatical to lead a mission for his church in Canada, recently moved to Alpine, Utah. He talked about the sense of community he felt when a group of people from his church volunteered to build the city a new park. Dave said he showed up with a rake and a shovel at 7 o'clock on a Saturday morning along with about 100 other people. "What do I know about building a park and cutting down trees? We all worked hard for 6 hours, and at the end of 6 hours there was a park. It sounds like we're back in the fifties, but that's kind of a nice thing for people to come together and give and help and do things." Dave added, reflecting on the importance of helping others, "There's that expression, on your gravestone they won't say what your title was or what your income was, they'll say who you cared about."

We believe that these kinds of experiences have allowed our interviewees to escape the psychophysical numbing we talked about in Chapter 3. Most of us, for example, when considering the millions of children orphaned by AIDS, sold into labor, exploited by the sex trade, or impoverished or diseased are numbed by the size and intensity of the problems. But our interviewees have life experiences that provide them concrete evidence of the difference they can make in the lives of individuals. Seeing the difference, as Sherri Kirkpatrick saw in the gift of a goat, allowed her to focus on the larger difference she makes in the lives of some children, rather than the overwhelming plight of all children. To Sherri, like all our interviewees, helping only one person is worth doing. It's a good place to be.

## Citizens of the World

Some of us live in rather small worlds, with only our own concerns at the center. When our thoughts, mental energies, curiosities, and sensitivities focus more externally, beyond ourselves, our own homes, even our own neighborhoods, our world expands. We are engaged in a larger world, and consequently a larger life. Harry Leibowitz expanded on this notion: "I thought I was sensitive to and understood a lot of the issues that face children in the world. I had no idea. I really never understood the depth of the problem of child sexual slavery and predation. I knew it was out there. I knew it was a problem. I never really understood how deep and difficult it was. In fact, one of the things I found so unusual is that in some countries the culture actually accepts it. It's not considered abnormal or illegal; it's not considered unethical. That was very hard for me to deal with."

Most people may be aware of these problems, in a safe, distant, clean-hands way. Our interviewees are not only aware, they are engaged, in an up-close, rolled-up-sleeves way. Rob Taylor, the firefighter from the Puget Sound area of Washington state, exemplifies this full-engagement approach. He talked about the satisfaction he has gained from his trips to Mexico, where he and his fellow churchgoers built houses for families in need. "As far as spiritual, it's just a soul-cleansing time for me. I guess more than anything, I learned just how wasteful we are in the United States and how much simpler life can be if you don't subscribe to the top-40 pop culture of the United States. It's not what life is. Life happens when you go out and do. I can't encourage people enough to share what you are good at with somebody else, or share even what you are willing to do with somebody else. It makes me feel good about life in general."

This "larger life" attitude now has Rob and his wife, Jennifer, traveling to different parts of the world, then adopting a young African girl, Rachael. As a result, the world becomes a little larger for their three sons as well. And this family's world will continue to expand. And we have just learned that Margaret Vernon went on to live and work in Rwanda after she completed her service in the Peace Corps. Most of our interviewees have traveled broadly, spent time in other cultures, sought out other peoples on quests or missions or labors of compassion. They are leading larger lives.

## No Regrets

Among the most significant sources of unhappiness about our life journeys are the regrets we have about choices we have made. Typically, the things we did not do are regretted much more than the things we did. As the American poet John Greenleaf Whittier wrote, "For of all sad words of tongue or pen, the saddest are these, 'it might have been.'" Our interviewees answered uniformly "no" when asked if they had made life choices they regretted.

Gerry Sieck, the corporate attorney turned teacher, told us he felt a deep sense of responsibility for helping children, "those who cannot help themselves." Reflecting on his decision to coach his daughter's basketball team, a decision that eventually led him to teaching school, Gerry said he made the only choice he could. "The fourth grade girls couldn't coach themselves. Why don't you guys get together and pick a coach—not an option. They needed an adult to raise their hand, and my hand went up. It had to go up."

Kathy Magee shared with us a self-awareness she experienced after returning from assisting with surgeries at four different sites in the Philippines. "When we came back it was Christmas time. I thought, I've got to get some Christmas presents. And that's when it really, definitely hit me. I went into the stores and was like, are you kidding me? I'm going to buy more clothes, more toys, anything for my kids? That's ridiculous. This world is off kilter here!" For Kathy, the contrast of a very poor country of people working in the rice paddies with the glitter of Christmas shopping was more than venial. "From that moment on we took high school students with us," Kathy said. "We now train high school students. They have clubs. We have more than 700 around the world, and we do a conference every summer that teaches them teamwork, leadership, how to work with cultures, as well as skits for them to teach primary health care."

We believe our interviewees have no regrets because they have each taken charge of their own lives. None of them has accepted, uncritically, lives that other people have crafted or designed for them. For better or worse—as far as we can tell, always better—our interviewees are creating their own futures.[6] They have made real-life choices. And for each of them, a different life has emerged. The choices took Liz Clibourne from Hawaii to Africa. They took Gerry Sieck from the boardroom to the classroom. They took Bill Sergeant from being fully retired to being fully engaged. They took Kathy Magee from familiar and expected surgical surroundings to the unexpected challenges and unfamiliar wonders of different cultures. In the end, there was no resumption of a normal day. Our interviewees have created new realities.

## The Path You Are On

You may be satisfied with the life you have, the path you are on. But perhaps you are considering a change in direction, however momentous or slight. Perhaps you are curious, or intrigued, by the paths taken by the people in this book. Maybe you'd like to veer off a little more in their direction.[7] We asked our interviewees what advice they would give to those considering such a change.

Bill Sergeant, the Rotarian who led the organization's effort to eradicate polio in the world, offered, "Everywhere I turn, I see people wanting help. In my city there are so many groups doing good things. I would say offer your services, because people, in my experience, are begging for help everywhere and almost any help that they can get."

Kathy Magee advised, "Rather than saying, I can't really do anything, I'll just write the check, call up that organization you think you could possibly do something for and say, these are my talents, I'd like to offer them. I'd like to come in and be a part of the team and do what I can do."

Harry Leibowitz suggested, "Cancer, Alzheimer's, your church, pick a cause that you feel passionate about. Then find somebody who is doing something in that genre and allow yourself to learn what they are doing. Get involved with them so you can see how it works."

Peter Samuelson, of the Starlight Children's Foundation, counseled, "Just do it. Don't allow anyone to tell you that it doesn't have value. That it's all too complicated. You just go do it. Then, miraculously, you see alternate paths, and you pursue them both, or three of them, or nine of them at once. And you don't know in advance which will work. Failure is fine; it leads to success."

Meg Campbell, the founder of a charter school for underprivileged children, posed a question: "What is the thing that you do that you lose track of time when you are doing it? Maybe you love to play the flute—there are just so many ways to make the world better, that's all. Go play the flute in the hospital if you love to play the flute. I do feel that if you really want pure happiness, whatever is your passion, you can take it to an exponential level of happiness by sharing it."

Rob Taylor had a complementary suggestion. "You don't have to go outside what you are capable of. You don't have to learn a new skill to be able to help. Most of the time you just find what you are good at and you can carve out your own niche."

And Lucy Helm said, "Talk to people who do what you're thinking of doing. What has motivated them? What has worked for them, how did they work it into their schedule? I think it is very reassuring when you realize that people can add volunteer work into their lives and it's not that difficult."

Margaret Vernon reminded us, "One thing that may help is to examine your priorities and see what kind of sacrifices you are willing to make. If you take too big of a step, it's just going to be negative for everyone involved. You're not going to want to finish it and the intended beneficiaries won't see the results. I would say that the first thing you need to do is to evaluate what you are willing to give up. Then just research the possibilities."

And Craig Kielburger offered a bit of advice that summarized many of the responses: "I am a big believer in a simple philosophy. Issue plus gift equals a better world. I think a lot of the time we make it very complicated, and it really isn't. We all have an issue we care about, something that gets us angry or concerned. Something close to home that maybe affects our family or maybe something we see on the news. All of us have something we want to change or better in our world. And then add to that your gift. We all have something that is unique to us, whether we are good at sports and we want to coach Little League or whether we are great when it comes to writing and want to share an issue for the local paper. Maybe we are compassionate listeners and we just go to a retirement home and give an ear to someone's stories. We all have very unique talents, and it's a question of just recognizing what we love to do naturally and then matching that with the issue. It's that simple."

Our interviewees were uniformly of an opinion that anyone can make a significant difference and that everyone has skills and talents that will be valued. Meg Campbell shared with us the story of an ornithologist who wanted to start a Saturday birding class at her charter school for lower-income children. "I have to admit I wasn't sure it would go over," Meg said. "The whole bird community is pretty much its own thing. I said to her, 'We'll put in a course description, but the children who are required to take a Saturday class get to choose which one, and I can't make them take this class.' So she put in the description—it was something about raptors and hawks—and she had eight boys sign up for this class. She's passionate about birds, and wouldn't you know it, I have eight boys now who are passionate about birds too. We have bird feeders; they have gone birding; they carry binoculars. They have no idea how nerdy this is." Meg added, "When anyone comes in and they want to volunteer at the school, I ask them what they're passionate about, because our need is so great that we can match them up with anything."

The suggestions coming from these extraordinary people all point to some straightforward questions we need to ask ourselves. What do I care about? What can I do or contribute? What am I willing to do? What is the first step? Our advice, as you answer these questions, is this: Pay attention to what is happening in your mind. Do things that might help you be more aware of what you are saying to yourself. Slow down the process. Make notes. Talk out loud to yourself. Talk to a friend. Externalize your thinking.[8] Why? Because when we are contemplating life choices, when we are choosing alternative pathways for the journey, there are some subtleties that, we believe, need to be more carefully examined.

## The Inner Debate

In the end, we come back to the question that Susie Scott Krabacher answered so affirmatively in the beginning of this book. Do I feel a sense of responsibility for helping others?[9] Because Susie said yes, countless lives in Haiti have been changed for the better. One of those is the life of a young boy named Kensen, who was found abandoned in a Port-au-Prince sewage canal.

"A street vendor selling her limited supply of vegetables saw his little hand come up above the water, and then she saw his nose bob just above the water and he went back down," Susie told us. "He was not quite 1-year-old. Someone had tied a cement block around his ankle and had thrown him into the sewage canal, but only after breaking all of the bones in his legs. The child was born with clubbed feet."

Susie explained the deliberate mangling was no doubt an attempt to break the feared curse on the family of this deformed child, an illegal but not uncommon practice in a society marked by superstition. Even before the earthquake that devastated the country in 2010, Haiti was desperately poor, and child abandonment was an enormous problem as parents were more likely to give up less-than-perfect children. AIDS, tuberculosis, and other infectious diseases were at alarmingly high rates, so the average life expectancy for anyone was low. More than three-quarters of the adult population was unemployed, and hunger was so pervasive children resorted to eating cookies made of dirt.[10] In this society on the threadbare fringe of civilization, an infant born with any defect, including clubbed feet, had a low chance of survivability right from the start.

"The street vendor enlisted the help of a passerby who pulled the child out, cut the rope tied to the cement block, and they carried the child to the government hospital," Susie continued. "That's where abandoned children go, and this child was obviously abandoned."

It was quickly discovered that the broken bones of the child had begun to heal, but were healing poorly. Fortunately, the government hospital had a close relationship with Mercy & Sharing, the orphanage founded by Susie that has taken over the care of abandoned children in Haiti. Mercy & Sharing managed to bring in and pay the doctors to fix the child's broken bones and put him in a body cast that extended above his waist.

"For a year, this child wouldn't smile," Susie recalled. "He was the most depressed, sad little boy that I had ever seen. He would just barely eat, just enough to stay alive. Most of the children, after we have them for 6 months, we can get them to giggle because they start getting used to their environment. He never even smiled."

One day, Susie told us, after the child had been in a body cast for a full year, a journalist was in town covering another story. She wanted to visit an orphanage, and her hotel recommended a visit to Mercy & Sharing. The journalist entered the orphanage with her camera and began taking pictures. Susie described this unexpected moment between the journalist and the boy. "He saw her, this single woman of the world, who had no interest in a family or marriage, he saw her and convulsed with laughter. I just don't know what it was. We told her he never smiled in his life and why he was in the body cast."

The journalist couldn't get the child out of her mind. She kept coming back to the orphanage. She even postponed her trip back home. After she arrived back home, she wrote Susie and asked, "Can I please adopt him?"

This story of a child who was born with clubbed feet, who was mangled and thrown away into a sewage canal, has a happy ending. "I get pictures all the time of Kensen wearing his new little tennis shoes with the lights on them," Susie said. "I thought he would always be depressed. But he is the happiest child ever. He is absolutely perfect."

Like that of all of our interviewees, Susie's contribution to Kensen's life, as well as to the larger human condition, may be traced back to the choices that preceded it. She chose to leverage her life experiences of abuse as a child into a sense of empathy for other children in need. This connection began when Susie saw in the eyes of a neglected child on television the same look she saw in the mirror as a young girl. She chose to see fairness in the world as an act of fate, not as an entitlement. Any one of us could have been born with clubbed feet into a superstitious culture. Because of her deep, emotional connection with abused children, she chose to believe she knew something and could do something that might just make a difference. She chose to be open to an opportunity to consider Haiti. She chose to take the first small step by visiting Haiti with a friend. When she encountered difficulties during her first few visits to Cité Soleil, she chose to persevere and stay with it. And she has chosen to lead the way by seeking the help of others through their involvement and charitable donations. Both Susie's life and the world we live in have benefited enormously because her choices have led her to helping the neglected children of Haiti.

Do I feel a sense of responsibility for helping others? The question is both critical and complex. It is critical because it defines our role in society. It is complex because either answer to the question, yes or no, carries a consequence. Here is where the internal struggle begins.[11]

If the answer is, "No, I am not responsible for helping those in need, pain, or peril," it tells us we are more narrowly focused. Such an answer may be bothersome in its implication. I eat while others starve. I have shelter while others sleep in the street. I am safe while others live in danger. My health needs are served while others are at risk.

On the other hand, if the answer is, "Yes, I am responsible for helping others," then a personal standard is created by which to conduct ourselves. And this yes answer requires us to do something. It creates the dense weight of personal responsibility. If I believe I am responsible for helping those in need and I do nothing, then I have not lived up to my own standard.[12]

Perhaps it is for this reason that the question is an easy one to avoid asking in the first place. It's easy to rationalize our way into believing we don't have to face the question because there is no point to it. We can tell ourselves the question is irrelevant because, whether we answer yes or no, we can't make a difference. But as we all know from experience, when it's just self and conscience in a low-profile debate, we can talk ourselves into or out of almost anything. We can conclude that we are helpless; that we have no choice; that we don't matter at all; that we will never do anything, ever, because no one can make a difference.

We see in our interviews a different way of thinking. It isn't immediately obvious. If it were obvious and straightforward thinking, it would not need to be so carefully culled for clues. Through the interview process, and our analyses of interview transcripts, we have deliberately decelerated the thinking of our interviewees long enough for them to ponder the perspectives underlying their own actions.

In searching for consistencies in how they see the world and themselves in it, we are able to understand how they think about their own relevance to society and others. Our interviewees offer a different way of talking to ourselves, bolstered by seven interlocking choice points. It is an inner path that can help turn a labyrinth of rationalization into a clear and intentional decision for assuming a more meaningful role in society and thereby a larger life.

Collectively, our interviewees provide a model for how we might moderate our own inner debate. Then, when we think about shaping our lives, we can arrive at an answer that is more authentic and true to how we see ourselves, or wish to be. We can quiet the din of rationalization so that we can hear what Mahatma Gandhi described as, "The still, small voice of conscience."

## Will Helping Others Make You Happier?

1. Writing in *Time* magazine, Nancy Gibbs concluded from recent research that "happiness correlates much more closely with our causes and connectedness than with our net worth." What do you think about this finding? Does this ring true in your own experience?

2. Why do you think there is so much attention now to the science of happiness, and what does this mean for your work? Do the new findings reinforce or challenge decisions you have made about your career or volunteer opportunities?

3. Each of our interviewees told us that making a difference in the lives of others improved his or her life as well. Can you give an example from your own experience of how helping others made your life happier or more fulfilling? Why do you think that was the case? What feelings did you have?

4. If helping others has also made our interviewees' lives happier, must we then conclude that altruism is ultimately a selfish act? Or, as some argue, is it a good thing that the doer of good also benefits because that will lead to more altruism in the world? (See this chapter's Note 4.) Do the motivations of the person who does good matter?

5. Many of our interviewees offered advice for others who want to get started helping others. From your experience, what suggestions would you offer? What worked for you when you were looking for a helping opportunity? Is it as simple as Craig Kielburger makes it when he says, "Issue plus gift equals a better world."

6. What is your perspective on the central question we ask at the end of this chapter: Do I feel a sense of responsibility for helping others? Why do you think some people choose to help those in need while others do not? Are there sometimes valid reasons for choosing not to help? Is giving money ever enough?

7. How would you like to be remembered? What would you want your legacy to be?

# 10

# Getting Started

*A Spectrum of Involvement*

If you want to make a difference in the world, you don't have to give a piece of your liver, address a major social problem like homelessness, or travel to a foreign country. There is an entire range of ways to make a difference, as illustrated in Figure 10.1. You can always determine your level of involvement. It's worth remembering that leaders like Larry Bradley, Inderjit Khurana, and Peter Samuelson didn't begin with solutions. They each began by learning about the challenge in front of them and worked their way toward a result.

If you're unsure of how to get started, you might find the following example useful. It offers a step-by-step approach to assuming increasing responsibility for a helping effort.

If you believe no one should go hungry, you can make a difference in a number of ways:

**1. What can I learn?** You could begin by learning about the food pantries and soup kitchens or Meals on Wheels programs in your local community. Being open to an opportunity begins with an external focus and knowing what is going on around you. A few phone calls or attending a meeting affords awareness.

**Figure 10.1**   Spectrum of Involvement

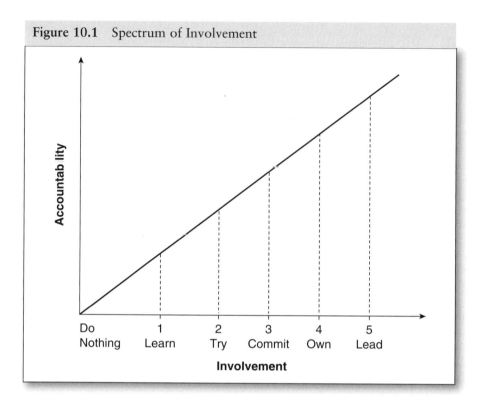

2. **I'll give it a try.** You may then try to contribute by serving food for a few hours at the soup kitchen or helping to hand out bags of groceries at the food pantry. You also could ride along with someone who delivers Meals on Wheels for the elderly and incapacitated to see if that is a way for you to contribute.

3. **Count on me.** You could offer to be part of the team of people who work at the kitchen or pantry. While you would commit your time, there would still be a number of people who could manage if you were unable to come.

4. **This has my name on it.** You could assume full accountability by owning a specific responsibility. For example, you could be the person who computerizes the inventory system at the food pantry or who takes responsibility for delivering meals along a specific route.

**5. I'll lead the way.** Finally, you could be the person who leads and manages the people and resources for any of these contributions to your community.

There are any number of ways to make a difference. You can start and you can stop. You can increase or decrease your responsibility at any time. Everything matters. Nothing is too small. You soon enough will arrive at a simple awareness: There is a vast difference between not enough and not at all. It all begins with choosing to do something.

Maybe you've been inspired to help others by some of the leaders profiled in this book. The following is a list of organizations associated with our interviewees, along with their websites if you'd like to get in touch.

### Adventures in Health, Education & Agricultural Development

*(aheadinc.org)*

### Bridges Across the Atlantic

*(hektoen.org / programs)*

### Camp Parkview

*(parkviewservices.org)*

### Center for the Protection of Children's Rights

*(humantrafficking.org)*

### Children to Children

*(childrentochildren.org)*

### City on a Hill Charter Public School

*(cityonahill.org)*

### Codman Academy Charter Public School

*(codmanacademy.org)*

**Every Child Every Village**

*(everychild-everyvillage.org)*

**Everyone Deserves a Roof**

*(edar.org)*

**First Star**

*(firststar.org)*

**Free The Children**

*(freethechildren.com)*

**Garden of Hope Foundation**

*(www.goh.org.tw/english)*

**HealthEd Connect**

*(healthedconnect.org)*

**Invest in Kids**

*(iik.org)*

**Lundy Foundation**

*(lundy-africa.org)*

**Mercy & Sharing**

*(haitichildren.org)*

**Multiple Myeloma Research Foundation**

*(themmrf.org)*

**OneChild Network**

*(onechild.ca)*

**Operation Smile**

*(operationsmile.org)*

**Peace Corps**

*(peacecorps.gov)*

**Rotary International**

*(rotary.org)*

**Ruchika Social Service Organization**

*(ruchika.org)*

**Ryan's Well Foundation**

*(ryanswell.ca)*

**Starlight Children's Foundation**

*(starlight.org)*

**World of Children**

*(worldofchildren.org)*

**Worldwide Orphans Foundation**

*(wwo.org)*

# Epilogue

## Beyond Our Research

*Without heroes we are all plain people and don't know how far we can go.*

—Bernard Malamud, *The Natural*

So what do we make of it all? We offer three thoughts.

First, there is a highly consistent composite profile among the 31 humanitarian leaders we interviewed for this book. While they are a diverse group and the contexts for their lives differ widely, there are no apparent outliers to the seven choice points emerging from their experiences, their perspectives, and their drive for making a difference in the lives of others. Unraveling each of their narratives, we see they have all traveled a remarkably similar path.

Second, they show us that helping others is not a backup plan for an unjust and inefficient society. It is at the core of what a just society is all about, allowing everyone to pursue a doable, constructive life as best as possible. In their own way, these humanitarian leaders help us imagine a different future. Without trumpeting the message, they give us a glimpse of a better way to conduct ourselves as a species, simply by seeing others through the best set of eyes possible: a human being in need. They show us being mindful of the question "What does the person in front of me need?" is perhaps the best sense of humanity a soul can express.

Third, they offer us a path for determining our own role in society, a path that makes helping those in need part of who we are. They show us that an enjoyable life and a meaningful life are not opposing aspirations. In fact, from their perspective, they are inseparable. Not only do our interviewees make a difference for others, but also for themselves, a difference they continue to absorb throughout their lives.

We seek the larger issues because they remind us we are more authentic than our daily to-do list might suggest. The larger issues make our lives larger. They allow us to be swept into new directions of meaningfulness that would otherwise go unimagined. When we are observant of the quality of life experienced by others, it makes us more alert to the quality of our own life.

When a thoughtful conscience examines itself, there is one question that is pivotal and answered whether or not we attend to it. What will be my place in the story of humanity? In other words, what is my passion? What is my role in society? What can I do to better the human condition? As we script the narrative of our life, we should imagine what we will look back on near the end of it all. There is wisdom in thinking it through sooner rather than later.

What will be your story?

# Appendix

## The Interview Process

Each interview followed a two-part process. At the outset, we told our interviewees we were first interested in learning about them as a person and second we were interested in learning about how they went about making their noteworthy contribution to helping others.

The first part of the interview focused on learning as much as possible about the person in terms of early childhood experiences, the significant people in their lives, their core values, as well as any events that may have shaped who they are as individuals. For this part of the interview, we were guided by the evaluation interview, a process of minimally guided conversation designed to promote an open and spontaneous discussion of important areas of interest and insights into personality, character, and underlying motivations. For this process we were guided by the long-standing work of Richard A. Fear and Robert J. Chiron in their book, *The Evaluation Interview*.

The second part of the interview focused on the contribution the interviewee made to helping others. For this part of the interview, we constructed 22 questions designed to help our interviewees provide a description of: why and how they decided to get involved in helping others; what occurred during their involvement; how their life may have been affected by the experience; and insights and recommendations for others wishing to get involved in helping people in need.

A. *Making the Decision to Get Involved*

1. How did you first become aware of the issue/problem/challenge?

2. How did you first become involved?

3. Why did you do this? Why was this important to you?

4. What convinced you that you were the right person to do this?

5. What led you to your decision to act? To get involved?

B. *During the Time of Involvement*

1. Did you encounter any obstacles along the way?

2. To what extent did this involve personal inconvenience or sacrifice?

3. How did you manage to involve other people?

4. What type of help or assistance did you get?

5. What do you think most helped you to succeed?

6. Do you remember a point in time when you felt unsure about your decision to get involved? What was happening?

7. Was there a point in time when you became convinced that this was the right thing for you to be doing?

C. *Reflections on the Experience*

1. What did you learn from this experience?

2. Has this experience changed you in any way?

3. What effect has this had on others that you might be aware of?

D. *Life Experiences and Personal Insights*

1. How might your life experiences have shaped or influenced your decision to act?

2. What are your feelings about the vast number of challenges in the world?

3. What is your perspective on fairness?

4. How do you know when you are stuck in complacency?

5. What do you do when you are afraid?

6. Is there a memorable story of success? Failure?

7. What would you recommend to others who want to act and make a difference but don't know how?

# Notes

## Introduction

1. Our basic criteria for selecting the 31 people were: (a) their actions were directed toward helping, assisting, or benefiting others; and (b) their helping behaviors were initiated for reasons other than self-interest. There is a continuing debate in the social sciences regarding the motivation for such humanitarian behavior, whether it is "selfish," in the sense that it satisfies some internal need or provides gratification. A long-standing researcher on empathy and altruism summarized his line of experimental research with the conclusion: "To the best of my knowledge, there is, at present, no plausible egoistic explanation of the cumulative evidence from these experiments," Batson (2010, p. 23). That is, empathic concern and the helpful behaviors that sometimes follow are associated with altruistic more than self-serving motivation.

2. Numerous theories of leadership have been developed over the past century. In the 5th edition of *Leadership: Theory and Practice* (2010), Peter G. Northouse presents an excellent summary and analysis of some of the more prominent theories and explores their practical applications.

3. In this updated edition of his leadership classic, Warren Bennis explores the transformative process through which people with certain qualities and competencies can become effective leaders (2003, p. xxviii).

4. Greenleaf (2002, p. 62). In conceptualizing humanitarian leadership, we were most influenced by the work of Robert Greenleaf, who introduced the theory of servant leadership in a seminal 1970 essay, *The Servant as Leader*. Greenleaf developed his ideas about leadership during a long career at AT&T, then the world's largest corporation. As Greenleaf explained in his essay: "The servant-leader is servant first. . . . It begins with the natural feeling that one wants to serve, to serve *first*. Then conscious choice brings

one to aspire to lead. That person is sharply different from one who is *leader* first, perhaps because of the need to assuage an unusual power drive or to acquire material possessions. . . . The leader-first and the servant-first are two extreme types. Between them there are shadings and blends that are part of the infinite variety of human nature," (2002, p. 27). Servant leadership has been embraced, examined, and elaborated on by many scholars and practitioners in the years since the idea was first introduced. It is a broad concept that has had far-reaching impact, leading to positive changes in corporate, educational, community, philanthropic, and other organizational cultures. (See Spears, 2002, for a collection of essays by prominent thinkers on servant leadership.) Although we were influenced by Greenleaf's concept of leaders whose primary purpose is to serve, our focus in this book is on leaders in less structured contexts, leaders whose relationships are not just with followers, but also, very importantly, with people in need.

5. The trait approach was one of the first attempts to study and understand the nature of leadership. Starting in the beginning of the 20th century, scholars looked for certain innate universal qualities that would differentiate leaders from nonleaders—sometimes called the "great man" theory. By mid-century, however, study had shifted to also understanding the kinds of situations leaders found themselves in, as well as their relationships with followers. The thinking was that leaders in one situation with a particular group of followers might not be leaders in another situation. The trait approach has generated renewed interest in recent years, with scholars once again focusing on the singular traits, such as emotional intelligence, that characterize effective leaders. See Northouse (2010) for a more complete discussion and analysis of the trait approach.

6. Grounded theory is a type of qualitative research often associated with a method of inquiry first developed in the 1960s by Barney Glaser and Anselm Strauss, sociologists who coined the term. It is a type of research more focused on discovery than verification. Rather than starting with a hypothesis that is then proved or disproved through research, grounded theory draws conclusions after research has been carried out. Grounded theory involves an iterative process in which data that are gathered—in this case through interviews—eventually lead to the formation of a theory through continual sampling and analysis. For a more complete discussion of grounded theory, see Glaser and Strauss (1967)and Strauss and Corbin (1990). For a helpful analysis of grounded theory, see Pidgeon (1996).

# Chapter 1

1. Victor Dukay's search for clarity or purpose has qualities that are common among individuals who have obtained "focus" for their lives. One analysis of such processes details their complexities. This analysis reminds us of the long and winding road we often must travel before the meaning or focus begins to take shape, and ends with the observation, "'Right' action thus conveys no sense of ultimate truth, but rather a sense of wholeness and completion, of matters clearly perceived and well-considered," Schaetti, Ramsey, & Watanabe (2008, p.127).

2. By *empathic connection* we mean that all of the people in our sample showed unequivocally either or both of two qualities: empathic concern or empathy (see Batson, 2010). Empathic concern is an emotional response to the perceived distress or need of the other. It is a feeling of compassion for another, and it's often called *sympathy*. Empathy is when you feel what another person feels; that is, your emotional response is the same as the other's emotional response to his or her distress or need. You feel pain, loss, despair, or fear.

3. Shamir and Eilam (2005) define authentic leaders as having "self-knowledge" and "self-concept clarity" (p. 402), and they argue that these leaders achieve this knowledge and clarity through the development of life stories. In constructing what Shamir and Eilam term a *self-narrative,* leaders draw connections between events in their lives that render these events coherent and understandable. Importantly, the researchers write, "Life stories provide authentic leaders with a self-concept that can be expressed through the leadership role. For instance, they provide the leader with knowledge and clarity about their values and convictions," (p. 402).

4. Summaries of theory and research on empathy, helping behaviors, and many related concepts are available in Mikulincer and Shaver (2010).

5. Mirror neurons were originally discovered in research on monkeys by Gallese, Fadiga, Fogassi, and Rizzolatti (1996).

6. For an account of how the new social neuroscience has informed theory and research on prosocial behavior, see Hein and Singer (2010).

7. For an explanation of mirror neurons that is accessible to a nonexpert but is written by a neuroscientist, see Iacoboni (2009).

8. One leadership theory, proposed by Robert Greenleaf and known as *servant leadership,* gives a central role to the kind of leadership that grows from the empathic connectedness between the leader and those he or she serves. See Spears (1998).

9. In fact, de Waal (2009) has traced the roots of empathy, and most human kindness, to our tendency to adopt the emotions and behavior of those we are close to, often parents.

10. Kouzes & Posner (1987, p. 25).

11. It's not at all unusual for adversity in one's life to be converted into spiritual growth, connectedness, and heightened introspection. Dillon and Wink (2007) have documented such processes in their 60-year longitudinal study of several hundred individuals.

12. Frankl (1984, p. 162).

## Chapter 2

1. In a review of the literature on empathy and fairness, Singer notes that both empathy and fairness "are social emotions arising only when embedded in the context of human interaction, and both point to the human being as altruistic, whether because he feels for the other or because he has a sense of social justice," (2007, p. 25). This conclusion was drawn after reviewing several studies linking the automatic neuronal response of empathy to the perception that someone was being treated unfairly. See Singer (2007, p. 25).

2. Park and Peterson (2003) identified six core virtues: justice, wisdom and knowledge, courage, love, transparence, and transcendence (connection to the larger universe or greater meaning).

3. According to one line of research summarized by Emmons (2010), if we recognize our good fortune and are predisposed toward "gratitude," we engage in helping behaviors like loaning money or providing emotional support more frequently than do less grateful people. Knowing we ourselves have been fortunate makes us more likely to help those who are less fortunate.

4. Gladwell (2008, p. 115).

5. Mayer (2007).

6. For a full description of Merton's theory of social structure and anomie, see Merton (1949/1968).

7. In *The Spirit Level: Why Greater Equality Makes Societies Stronger* (2009), Wilkinson and Pickett analyze internationally comparable information on income and income distribution, as well as data on an array of health and social problems. This information, from the United Nations, World Bank, World Health Organization, U.S. Census, and other reputable sources, has only recently become available. The researchers' analysis enabled them to develop a series of scatter graphs

linking income inequality within societies to various health and social ills. The graphs show these relationships either internationally, comparing rich countries, or in the United States, comparing different states. The researchers wanted to understand how societies can make further improvements to the quality of human life at a time when real benefits from economic growth in many affluent countries may be coming to an end. The answer they suggest is greater equality. They write that "we are affected very differently by the income differences within our own society from the way we are affected by the differences in average income between one rich society and another," (p. 11). What matters in determining health and social well-being, they found in comparing data from the richest countries, is not the average income in a society, but the degree of income disparity between people within a society. Their analysis explains, for example, why the United States, one of the world's richest countries but also one with wide disparities in income, has the lowest longevity of any developed nation and also alarmingly high levels of violence. Wilkinson and Pickett conclude that everyone's human potential is diminished in one way or another in an unequal society.

## Chapter 3

1. Even the worst imaginable environments in which very young children find themselves can be overcome by the efforts of caring individuals. See, for example, Benoit, Jocelyn, Moddemann, and Embree (1996).

2. The quality we describe as "believe we can matter" is very much akin to self-efficacy beliefs. One study, done in Italy, found that the perception that one can help, along with personal values that are in opposition to self-enhancement (achievement and power) predict behaviors such as helping and caring for others. See Caprara and Steca (2007).

3. This phenomenon is described by Fetherstonhaugh, Slovic, Johnson, and Friedrich (1997). How this effect manifests itself in, for example, donations to victim causes can be seen in Small, Lowenstein, and Slovic (2007).

4. Research on supporting political activism and donating to the Humane Society has suggested that the more individualized the appeal the more likely donations and support are to increase. See Keum and colleagues (2005) and Perrine and Heather (2000).

5. Nicholas Kristof (2009) writes frequently on humanitarian issues for the *New York Times*. Paul Slovic (2007) is a pioneer in the study of psychic numbing.

6. A very compelling body of research on early childhood development demonstrates that early "lessons," especially those accompanied by unobtrusive (e.g., modeling versus directing or criticizing) behavior, can have significant effects on "a variety of motivation-related outcomes," Shonkoff & Phillips (2000, p. 157). This brief story told by Gerry Sieck is a graphic illustration of this research finding.

7. In its comprehensive form, contingency theory involves three components. As Fiedler describes, "Under normal conditions, the leader who is liked and accepted by his group (or feels liked and accepted), who has high position power, and who has a clear-cut task, has everything in his favor," (1967, pp. 142–143).

8. The ability to envision two futures is by no means a given. In fact, we contend that the recognition, or knowledge, that you *can* change the future for others, and for yourself, immediately changes "the complexity of the on-going problem-solving mental process," a quality that Jaques and Cason have researched extensively and find to be a key concept in explaining an individual's *potential capability*. See Jaques & Cason (1994, p. 20).

# Chapter 4

1. Miriam Lewin, daughter of Kurt Lewin (1890–1947), notes that her father often said, "the best way to obtain a theoretical understanding of a phenomenon is to try to change it." See Lewin (1998). Edgar H. Schein, professor of management emeritus at the MIT Sloan School of Management, discusses the thinking that underpins this quotation by Kurt Lewin in a 1995 essay.

2. Keltner (2009, p. x).

3. Maslow describes what has become a classic theory of human motivation expressed through a hierarchy of basic needs. As lower-level needs are satisfied, higher-level needs arise, with physiological needs being at the lowest level. For individuals to focus on needs external to themselves, self-needs for physiological functioning, safety, belonging, and love and esteem have to first be met. This allows an individual to develop the need for self-actualization. Self-actualized individuals "are in general strongly focused on problems outside themselves. In current terminology they are problem centered rather than ego centered," (1954, p. 211).

# Chapter 5

1. Craig spoke often of his brother, Marc, and the supportive home environment provided by his parents. This interview and the book authored by Craig and Marc (Kielburger & Kielburger, 2006) epitomized for us an important scientific discovery. This discovery was summarized by the Committee on Integrating the Science of Early Childhood Development in their landmark work. The committee emphasized fostering "the capacity to experience the enhanced motivation associated with feeling competent and loved," Shonkoff & Phillips (2000, p. 5).

2. Courage may well be a central component in the X factor in leadership, alluded to by one of the most highly recognized leadership scholars, James MacGregor Burns (2003). An element of risk, sometimes danger, can be found in the initial leadership acts of our sample of leaders.

3. This action orientation has been found in, for example, Bennis and Nanus's (1985) research; in Kouzes and Posner's (1987) research; in our own research, LaFasto and Larson (2001), and in the more recent contribution to contemporary leadership theory, Heifetz, Grashow, and Linsky (2009).

4. Our observation is consistent with one advanced in an analysis of a wide range of organization "forms" and concludes that people often act from an emotional and intuitive sense of what is "right." See Worline and Quinn (2003).

5. Merton began his explanation of the self-fulfilling prophecy by stating, "In a series of works seldom consulted outside the academic fraternity, W. I. Thomas, the dean of American sociologists, set forth a theorem basic to the social sciences: 'If men define situations as real, they are real in their consequences,'" (1949/1968, p. 475.)

# Chapter 6

1. Martin Seligman's work suggests that among the virtues that are universally admired is perseverance, which exemplifies courage, a virtue present in the heroes of "every culture," (2002, p.145).

2. In reporting their results, Duckworth, Peterson, Matthews, and Kelly (2007, p. 1098) state, "Across six studies, individual differences in grit accounted for significant incremental variance in success outcomes over and beyond that explained by IQ, to which it was not positively related."

## Chapter 7

1. Burns (1978, p. 20). James MacGregor Burns, a seminal thinker in the field of transformational leadership, is also a Pulitzer Prize–winning presidential biographer.

2. For a summary of the historical, clinical, and biological evidence that emotions and behavior are contagious, see Brennan (2004). For an accessible explanation of the social neurology of emotional contagion, see Goleman (2006). The evidence is noteworthy not so much for proof of the *fact* that emotions and behavior are contagious between people, but for evidence of the degree or *extent* to which emotions and behavior from one person change the internal makeup, from neuronal to physiological, of the other.

3. The attitudinal climate of the early stakeholder groups (belief in and commitment to the process, motivation to impact the root problem, and so on) transferred to the administrators of the nurse-home visitation programs, then to the nurses working with young mothers, and significantly impacted the mothers' commitment to and longevity in the program. See Hicks, Larson, Nelson, Olds, and Johnston (2008).

4. Burns (1978, p. 4).

## Chapter 8

1. Figure 8.1 is visually patterned after Kurt Lewin's concept of force field analysis, a framework for analyzing the opposing driving and restraining forces that impact change. See Lewin (1947). For a helpful discussion of force field analysis, see Schein (1995).

2. In *Leadership Without Easy Answers* (1994), Heifetz differentiates between technical and adaptive problems and argues that each requires a different kind of leadership. He classifies situations as Type I, II, or III. Type I situations are the easiest to address; they are technical in nature and have a clear problem definition, as well as a clear solution and implementation. In Type II situations, which he classifies as technical and adaptive, the problem definition is clear, but the solution and implementation require learning. In Type III situations, the most difficult, the problem definition, as well as the solution and implementation require learning. Type III situations require adaptive work, according to Heifetz. Leaders must "induce learning" so that the gap is diminished between the values people hold and the reality they face.

# Chapter 9

1. The research on happiness typically finds positive correlations between prosocial behavior (e.g., helping others, performing altruistic acts) and happiness. See Lyubomirsky, King, and Diener (2005). The direction of the causal relationship can be argued both ways, but our interviewees perceive their helping behavior as having made them happy.

2. Gibbs (2009, p. 116).

3. Fowler and Christakis (2009, p. 23).

4. Beyond Batson's work on the possible underlying motivations for altruism, which is referenced in Note 1 of the Introduction, Judith Lichtenberg (2010), professor of philosophy at Georgetown University, offers an excellent extended discussion of whether pure altruism is possible since so many acts of goodness benefit the doer of good as well as the beneficiary.

5. Even though good work may occur in difficult times, amid pain and suffering, it nevertheless promotes positive emotions in the person doing the good work. See Gardner, Csikszentmihalyi, and Damon (2001, p. 5).

6. We have already presented interviewee statements and citations to other research that demonstrate connections between giving, or altruism, and subjective well-being. Research on the life-outcomes of giving also has found that it contributes to good physical and mental health, as well as lower mortality. See Post and Neimark (2007).

7. For additional examples of how people have chosen various paths of giving, see Fraser and Spizman (2009). Insight and experienced advice on multiple ways of making a difference in the lives of others is offered by Bronfman and Solomon (2010). President Bill Clinton, whose giving has impacted many root problems, especially the global AIDS efforts, offers his advice in *Giving: How Each of Us Can Change the World* (2007). If you are interested in learning about up-to-date developments on this topic, see the online publication, *Greater Good Magazine*, at http://greatergood-berkeley.edu/.

8. Even gross differences among us, such as in hope or optimism, are mediated by greater consciousness. Being clear about your behavioral intentions can promote both higher levels of action and more focused action. One research article that synthesized several studies concluded, "Taken together, the prior research and the present studies converge to indicate that high optimists have more active self-regulatory lives than do their less positive counterparts." See Geers, Wellman, and Lassiter (2009, p. 930).

9. Prior research tells us that this reflection on our own responsibility for helping others usually involves some aspects of (a) *accountability*—I will directly determine the outcomes for the person in need; (b) *role requirements*—I should help as a parent, friend, teacher, nurse, etc.; (c) *distinctive suitability*—I have the right skills, resources, etc.; and (d) *direct appeals*—I am being asked for a good reason. See Schwartz (1977).

10. Katz (2008).

11. Evidence from history, human evolution, and the new discipline of social neuroscience has led Keltner, in his book *Born to Be Good* (2009, p. 226), to conclude that, "The ebb and flow of marriages, families, friends, and workplaces track the dynamic tension between these two great forces—raw self-interest and a devotion to the welfare of the other."

12. This sense of individual guilt, or disappointment with oneself, is present in most, if not all, cultures, especially those that have strong religious traditions. A willingness to help those in need is often an internalized standard for being a "good" person. See Trout (2009).

# References

Batson, C. D. (2010). Empathy-induced altruistic motivation. In M. Mikulincer & P. R. Shaver (Eds.), *Prosocial motives, emotions, and behavior: The better angels of our nature* (pp. 15–34). Washington DC: American Psychological Association.

Bennis, W. (2003). *On becoming a leader.* New York: Basic Books.

Bennis, W., & Nanus, B. (1985). *Leaders: The strategies for taking charge.* New York: Harper & Row.

Benoit, T., Jocelyn, L., Moddemann, D., & Embree, J. (1996). Romanian adoption: The Manitoba experience. *Archives of Pediatrics and Adolescent Medicine, 150*(12), 1278–1283.

Brennan, T. (2004). *The transmission of affect.* Ithaca, NY: Cornell University Press.

Bronfman, C., & Solomon, J. (2010). *The art of giving: Where the soul meets a business plan.* San Francisco: Jossey-Bass.

Burns, J. M. (1978). *Leadership.* New York: Harper Torchbooks, Harper & Row.

Burns, J. M. (2003). *Transforming leadership.* New York: Grove Press.

Caprara, G. V., & Steca, P. (2007). Prosocial agency: The contribution of values and self-efficacy beliefs to prosocial behavior across ages. *Journal of Social and Clinical Psychology, 26*(2), 218–239.

Clinton, B. (2007). *Giving: How each of us can change the world.* New York: Alfred A. Knopf.

Dillon, M., & Wink, P. (2007). *In the course of a lifetime: Tracing religious belief, practice, and change.* Berkeley: University of California Press.

de Waal, F. (2009). *The age of empathy: Nature's lessons for a kinder society.* New York: Harmony.

Duckworth, A., Peterson, C., Matthews, M., & Kelly, D. (2007). Grit: Perseverance and passion for long-term goals. *Journal of Personality and Social Psychology, 92*(6), 1087–1101. doi: 10.1037/0022-3514.92.6.1087

Emmons, R. (2010). Pay it forward. In D. Keltner, J. Marsh, & J. Smith (Eds.), *The compassionate instinct* (pp. 77–85). New York: W.W. Norton.

Fear, R. A., & Chiron, R. J. (2002). *The evaluation interview* (5th ed.). New York: McGraw-Hill.

Fetherstonhaugh, D., Slovic, P., Johnson, S. M., & Friedrich, J. (1997). Insensitivity to the value of human life: A study of psychophysical numbing. *Journal of Risk and Uncertainty, 14*(3), 283–300.

Fiedler, F. (1967). *A theory of leadership effectiveness.* New York: McGraw-Hill.

Fowler, J. H., & Christakis, N. A. (2009). Dynamic spread of happiness in a large social network: Longitudinal analysis over 20 years in the Framingham Heart Study. *British Medical Journal, 338*(7685), pp. 23–27. doi: 10.10.1136/bmj.a2338

Frankl, V. E. (1984). *Man's search for meaning.* New York: Washington Square Books. (Original work published 1946)

Fraser, E., & Spizman, R. (2009). *Do your giving while you are living: Inspirational lessons on what you can do today to make a difference tomorrow.* New York: Morgan James.

Gallese, V., Fadiga, L., Fogassi, L., & Rizzolatti, G. (1996). Action recognition in the premotor cortex. *Brain, 119*(2), 593–609.

Gardner, H., Csikszentmihalyi, M., & Damon, W. (2001). *Good work: When excellence and ethics meet.* New York: Basic Books.

Geers, A., Wellman, J., & Lassiter, G. (2009). Dispositional optimism and engagement: The moderating influence of goal prioritization. *Journal of Personality and Social Psychology, 96*(4), 913–932. doi: 10.1037/a0014830

Gibbs, N. (2009, November 23). The happiness paradox: Why are Americans so cheery. *Time, 174*(20), p. 116.

Gladwell, M. (2008). *Outliers: The story of success.* New York: Little, Brown.

Glaser, B., & Strauss, A. (1967). *The discovery of grounded theory: Strategies for qualitative research.* New York: Aldine.

Goleman, D. (2006). *Social intelligence: The new science of human relationships.* New York: Random House.

Greenleaf, R. (2002). *Servant leadership: A journey into the nature of legitimate power & greatness* (25th anniversary ed., L. Spears, Ed.). Mahwah, NJ: Paulist Press.

Heifetz, R. (1994). *Leadership without easy answers.* Cambridge, MA: Harvard University Press.

Heifetz, R., Grashow, A., & Linsky, M. (2009). *The practice of adaptive leadership.* Boston: Harvard Business Press.

Hein, G., & Singer, T. (2010). Neuroscience meets social psychology: An integrated approach to human empathy and prosocial behavior. In M. Mikulincer & P. R. Shaver (Eds.), *Prosocial motives, emotions, and behavior: The better angels of our nature* (pp. 109–125). Washington, DC: American Psychological Association.

Hicks, D., Larson, C., Nelson, C., Olds, D. L., & Johnston, E. (2008). The influence of collaboration on program outcomes. *Evaluation Review, 32*(5), 453–477. doi: 10.1177/0193841X08315131

Iacoboni, M. (2009). *Mirroring people: The science of empathy and how we connect with others.* New York: Picador.

Jaques, E., & Cason, K. (1994). *Human capability: A study of individual potential and its application.* Falls Church, VA: Cason Hall.

Katz, J. (2008, January 30). Rising costs force Haiti's poor to eat dirt. *USA Today.* Retrieved from http://www.usatoday.com./news/world/2008-01-30-haiti-poor_N.htm

Keltner, D. (2009). *Born to be good: The science of a meaningful life.* New York: W.W. Norton.

Keum, H., Hillback, E. D., Rojas, H., De Zuniga, H. G., Shah, D. V., & McLeold, D. M. (2005). Personifying the radical: How news framing polarizes security concerns and tolerance judgments. *Human Communication Research, 31*(3), 337–364.

Kielburger, C., & Kielburger, M. (2006). *Me to we: Finding meaning in a material world.* New York: Fireside.

Kouzes, J., & Posner, B. (1987). *The leadership challenge.* San Francisco: Jossey-Bass.

Krabacher, S. S. (2007). *Angels of a lower flight.* New York: Simon & Schuster.

Kristof, N. (2009, July 9). Would you let this girl drown? *New York Times.* Retrieved from http://www.nytimes.com/2009/07/09/opinion/09kristof.html

LaFasto, F., & Larson, C. (2001). *When teams work best.* Thousand Oaks, CA: Sage.

Larson, C., & LaFasto, F. (1989). *TeamWork.* Newbury Park, CA: Sage.

Lewin, K. (1947). Group decision and social change. In T. M. Newcomb & E. L. Hartley (Eds.), *Readings in social psychology* (pp. 340–344). New York: Holt.

Lewin, M. (1998). Kurt Lewin: His psychology and his daughter's recollections. In G. A. Kimble & R. Wertheimer (Eds.), *Portraits of pioneers in psychology.* Washington, DC: American Psychological Association.

Lichtenberg, J. (2010, October 19). Is pure altruism possible? *New York Times.* Retrieved from http://opinionator.blogs.nytimes.com/2010/10/19/is-pure-altruism-possible?

Lyubomirsky, S., King, L., & Diener, E. (2005). The benefits of frequent positive affect: Does happiness lead to success? *Psychological Bulletin, 131*(6), 803–855.

Maslow, A. (1954). *Motivation and personality*. New York: Harper & Row.

Mayer, C. (2007, May 10). Gordon Brown: The Time interview. *Time.* Retrieved from http://www.time.com/time/world/article/0,8599,1619197,00.html

Merton, R. K. (1968). *Social theory and social structure* (Rev. ed.). New York: Free Press. (Original work published 1949)

Mikulincer, M., & Shaver, P. R. (Eds.). (2010). *Prosocial motives, emotions, and behavior: The better angels of our nature*. Washington, DC: American Psychological Association.

Northouse, P. (2010). *Leadership: Theory and practice* (5th ed.). Thousand Oaks, CA: Sage.

Park, N., & Peterson, C. (2003). Virtues and organizations. In K. Cameron, J. Dutton, & R. Quinn (Eds.), *Positive organizational scholarship: Foundations of a new discipline* (pp. 33–47). San Francisco: Berrett-Koehler.

Perrine, R. M., & Heather, S. (2000). Effects of picture and even-a-penny-will-help appeals on anonymous donations to charity. *Psychological Reports, 86*(2), 551–559.

Pidgeon, N. (1996). Grounded theory: Theoretical background. In T. E. Richardson (Ed.), *Handbook of qualitative research methods for psychology and the social sciences* (pp. 75–101). Oxford, UK: The British Psychological Society.

Post, S., & Neimark, J. (2007). *Why good things happen to good people*. New York: Broadway Books.

Schaetti, B., Ramsey, S., & Watanabe, G. (2008). *Personal leadership: Making a world of difference*. Seattle, WA: FlyingKite.

Schein, E. H. (1995). Kurt Lewin's change theory in the field and in the classroom: Notes toward a model of managed learning. Retrieved from http://www.solonline.org/res/wp/10006.html

Schwartz, S. H. (1977). Normative influences on altruism. In L. Berkowitz (Ed.), *Advances in experimental social psychology, Vol. 10* (pp. 221–270). New York: Academic Press.

Seligman, M. E. P. (2002). *Authentic happiness*. New York: Free Press.

Shamir, B., & Eilam, G. (2005). "What's your story?" A life-stories approach to authentic leadership development. *The Leadership Quarterly, 16*, 395–417.

Shonkoff, J., & Phillips, D. (Eds). (2000). *From neurons to neighborhoods: The science of early childhood development.* Washington, DC: National Academy Press.

Singer, T. (2007). The neuronal basis of empathy and fairness. In G. Bock & J. Goode (Eds.), *Empathy and fairness* (pp. 20–40). Chichester, UK: Wiley.

Slovic, P. (2007). "If I look at the mass I will never act": Psychic numbing and genocide. *Judgment and Decision Making, 2*(2), 79–95.

Small, D., Lowenstein, G., & Slovic, P. (2007). Sympathy and callousness: The impact of deliberative thought on donations to identifiable and statistical victims. *Organizational Behavior and Human Decision Processes, 102*(2), 143–153. doi: 10.1016/j.obhdp.2006.01.005

Spears, L. C. (Ed.). (1998). *Insights on leadership: Service, stewardship, spirit, and servant-leadership.* New York: Wiley.

Spears, L. C. (Ed.). (2002). *Focus on leadership: Servant leadership for the twenty-first century.* New York: Wiley.

Stoneham, N. (2004, June 8). Child protection special: Part one. *Bangkok Post.* Retrieved from http://www.bangkokpost.com/education/site2004/cvjn0804.htm

Strauss, A., & Corbin, J. (1990). *Basics of qualitative research: Grounded theory procedures and techniques.* Thousand Oaks, CA: Sage.

The 2011 Time 100. (2011, May 2). *Time,* pp. 37–154.

Trout, J. D. (2009). *The empathy gap: Building bridges to the good life and the good society.* London: Viking Penguin.

Wilkinson, R., & Pickett, K. (2009). *The spirit level: Why greater equality makes societies stronger.* New York: Bloomsbury.

Worline, M., & Quinn, R. (2003). Courageous principled action. In K. Cameron, J. Dutton, & R. Quinn (Eds.). *Positive organizational scholarship* (pp. 138–161). San Francisco: Berrett-Koehler.

# Photo Credits

The photographs in this book are used by permission and courtesy of the following individuals and organizations (page numbers refer to the photographic insert):

Page 1: Dr. Irving and Elvira Williams

Pages 2–3: Larry Bradley

Page 4: Kathy Sergeant

Page 5: Kathryn Funderburk

Page 6: Cheryl Perera, top; © Kit Williams, courtesy of Jennifer Atler, bottom

Page 7: Ryan's Well Foundation

Pages 8–9: Free The Children

Page 10: Jane Aronson, top; Dave Ulrich, bottom

Page 11: Makenzie Snyder

Pages 12–13: Dr. David J. Winchester

Page 14: Father Gary Graf

Page 15: Lucy Helm, top; Gerry Sieck, bottom

Page 16: Kathy Giusti

Page 17: Sanphasit Koompraphant

Pages 18–19: Harry Leibowitz

Page 20: Anoop Khurana

Page 21: Victor Dukay

Page 22: Sherri Kirkpatrick

Page 23: Peter Samuelson

Page 24: Liz Clibourne

Page 25: Operation Smile photos by Marc Ascher

Page 26: Hui-jung Chi

Page 27: Margaret Vernon

Page 28: Rob Taylor

Page 29: Photo by Peter Vanderwarker, courtesy of Meg Campbell

Page 30: Mike and Tracey Goffman

Page 31: Susie Scott Krabacher

Page 32: Victor Dukay

# Index

# Acknowledgments

This book would not have been possible without the participation, wisdom, support, and expertise of many individuals. First and foremost, we are deeply indebted to the 31 extraordinary people we interviewed for our research. For the privilege of sharing the stories of their lives and the candor with which they revealed them, we are genuinely grateful. Sadly, two of the people we profiled, Inderjit Khurana and Bill Sergeant, both giants of humanitarian leadership, passed away after we had completed our interviews. We extend our sincere thanks to their families for contributing photographs and reviewing the manuscript on Inderjit's and Bill's behalf.

We are grateful to the following editors, who ably assisted us with the development, editing, and production of this book. Lisa Shaw, senior executive editor at SAGE Publications, provided experienced and knowledgeable guidance every step of the way, and she did it with relentless good humor. Most important, Lisa believed in this book from the moment she read an early draft of the manuscript. MaryAnn Vail, assistant editor at SAGE, was very helpful in securing expert reviews of our manuscript and consolidating the feedback. Eric Garner, production editor, was consistently collaborative, responsive, and knowledgeable in shepherding the book through the complex production process. In addition, Gail Buschman created a cover design that embraced the multidimensional themes and values in this book and was committed to addressing every artistic challenge along the way.

Liz Rimer, our long-time development editor, contributed diligent research, sharp thinking about every issue and idea, as well as skillful editing. We are grateful for her unflagging commitment to this project from day one to completion. John Bergez, a gifted editor, offered meaningful and pragmatic suggestions. Trey Thoelcke was a meticulous and thoughtful copyeditor.

We are deeply indebted to our wives and children, who contributed to our research, read the manuscript, and offered sound advice and needed encouragement. Barbara LaFasto, whose wise perspective was formed through years of volunteer work at a food pantry, soup kitchen, and Meals on Wheels, served as a pragmatic beacon of guidance. Barbara also provided numerous insightful reviews of the manuscript and technical expertise in digitally creating the layout for the photographs. Sarah LaFasto offered a careful review of an early manuscript from a young person's point of view, as well as creative ideas for the cover design of the book.

Catherine Sweeney reviewed the manuscript and provided reliable guidance on the interpretation of several leadership theories. Laurie Larson contributed her superb skills with the review and synthesis of outside research on subjects critical to the conceptual understandings offered in this book.

Geri Schulz has played a unique role throughout the development of this and our two previous books. Geri is a talented assistant with the kind of positive attitude and can-do spirit that makes work a pleasure. Geri's work is impeccable, but just as important, she approaches every challenge with the attitude that nothing is impossible. We are deeply thankful to Geri for her cheerful involvement throughout this project.

Several trusted friends and colleagues provided welcome assistance and feedback as we developed the manuscript. Steve Griffin conducted a helpful literature search in the early research phase of this project. Pam Volk's perspective helped shape our approach to the reader. Geoffrey Fenton offered useful input into narrating the story of one of our interviewees. Father Gosbertus Rwezahura assisted with the translation of the Swahili phrases in this book.

We are particularly grateful to Peter Northouse, whose comprehensive leadership text and astute review of our manuscript helped place our work within the larger context of leadership research.

We also wish to thank Cardinal Health, Inc., for their support during the early stages of this project.

A very special thank you goes to Harry Leibowitz, the founder, along with his wife, Kay, of World of Children. Without hesitation,

Harry encouraged numerous World of Children awardees to partici-
pate as interviewees in our research. The longevity of their work as
humanitarians made them extremely valuable to our study and
strengthened our confidence in our findings. Also at World of
Children, Annette Andre helped facilitate ongoing communication
with our interviewees.

Finally, to everyone mentioned above and others who participated
in this project in ways both large and small, you have our deep and
lasting gratitude.

# About the Authors

Frank LaFasto                    Carl Larson

**Frank LaFasto**, Ph.D., and **Carl Larson**, Ph.D., have worked together on research in the areas of teamwork, leadership, and collaboration for nearly 40 years. They coauthored two best-selling books, *TeamWork: What Must Go Right/What Can Go Wrong* (SAGE Publications, 1989) and *When Teams Work Best: 6,000 Team Members and Leaders Tell What It Takes to Succeed* (SAGE Publications, 2001).

Frank recently retired as Senior Vice President of Organization Effectiveness after 30 years with Cardinal Health, Inc., a multinational health care company. An internationally recognized author and lecturer on leadership and management, Frank has more than 35 years' experience helping organizations build and sustain successful teams and develop executive talent. He currently consults with private and public sector organizations and with nonprofit groups. Frank resides in Lake Forest, Illinois.

Carl is Professor Emeritus of Human Communication Studies and past Dean of Social Sciences at the University of Denver. In 1997, Carl received the Driscoll Master Educator Award given by students at the University of Denver to the university's outstanding professor. Carl's main research activities focus on groups and teams, and on negotiation and collaborative processes. He consults extensively in both the private and public sectors. In addition to the two books on teamwork that he coauthored with Frank LaFasto, Carl is the coauthor of five other books on human communication. Carl lives in Denver, Colorado.

# SAGE Research Methods Online

## The essential tool for researchers

**Sign up now at www.sagepub.com/srmo for more information.**

### An expert research tool

- An **expertly designed taxonomy** with more than 1,400 unique terms for social and behavioral science research methods

- **Visual and hierarchical search tools** to help you discover material and link to related methods

- Easy-to-use navigation tools
- Content organized by complexity
- Tools for citing, printing, and downloading content with ease
- Regularly updated content and features

### A wealth of essential content

- The most comprehensive picture of quantitative, qualitative, and mixed methods available today

- More than **100,000 pages of SAGE book and reference material** on research methods as well as editorially selected material from SAGE journals

- More than **600 books** available in their entirety online

**Launching 2011!**

ⓈSAGE research methods online